Freedom's Soldiers

When nearly 200,000 black men, most of them former slaves, entered the Union army and navy, they transformed the Civil War into a struggle for liberty and changed the course of American history. *Freedom's Soldiers* tells the story of those men in their own words and the words of other eyewitnesses. These moving letters, affidavits, and memorials—drawn from the records of the National Archives—reveal the variety and complexity of the African-American experience during the era of emancipation.

FREEDOM: A DOCUMENTARY HISTORY OF
EMANCIPATION, 1861–1867,
4 vols. to date (Cambridge University Press, 1982–)

Series 1, volume 1, THE DESTRUCTION OF SLAVERY, ed. Ira Berlin, Barbara J. Fields, Thavolia Glymph, Joseph P. Reidy, and Leslie S. Rowland (1985).

Series 1, volume 2, THE WARTIME GENESIS OF FREE LABOR: THE UPPER SOUTH, ed. Ira Berlin, Steven F. Miller, Joseph P. Reidy, and Leslie S. Rowland (1993).

Series 1, volume 3, THE WARTIME GENESIS OF FREE LABOR: THE LOWER SOUTH, ed. Ira Berlin, Thavolia Glymph, Steven F. Miller, Joseph P. Reidy, Leslie S. Rowland, and Julie Saville (1990).

Series 2, THE BLACK MILITARY EXPERIENCE, ed. Ira Berlin, Joseph P. Reidy, and Leslie S. Rowland (1982).

SLAVES NO MORE: THREE ESSAYS ON EMANCIPATION
AND THE CIVIL WAR
by Ira Berlin, Barbara J. Fields, Steven F. Miller, Joseph P. Reidy, and Leslie S. Rowland (Cambridge University Press, 1992).

FREE AT LAST: A DOCUMENTARY HISTORY OF
SLAVERY, FREEDOM, AND THE CIVIL WAR
ed. Ira Berlin, Barbara J. Fields, Steven F. Miller, Joseph P. Reidy, and Leslie S. Rowland (The New Press, 1992).

FAMILIES AND FREEDOM: A DOCUMENTARY HISTORY OF
AFRICAN-AMERICAN KINSHIP IN THE CIVIL WAR ERA
ed. Ira Berlin and Leslie S. Rowland (The New Press, 1997).

FREEDOM'S SOLDIERS

THE BLACK MILITARY EXPERIENCE
IN THE CIVIL WAR

Edited by
IRA BERLIN
JOSEPH P. REIDY
LESLIE S. ROWLAND

CAMBRIDGE
UNIVERSITY PRESS

PUBLISHED BY THE PRESS SYNDICATE OF THE UNIVERSITY OF CAMBRIDGE
The Pitt Building, Trumpington Street, Cambridge CB2 1RP, United Kingdom

CAMBRIDGE UNIVERSITY PRESS
The Edinburgh Buidling, Cambridge CB2 2RU, UK   http://www.cup.cam.ac.uk
40 West 20th Street, New York, NY 10011-4211, USA   http://www.cup.org
10 Stamford Road, Oakleigh, Melbourne 3166, Australia

© Ira Berlin, Joseph P. Reidy, and Leslie S. Rowland   1998

First published 1998

Printed in the United States of America

Typeset in Garamond 3 and Palatino

*A catalog record for this book is available from
the British Library.*

Library of Congress Cataloging-in-Publication data is available.

ISBN 0 521 63258 7 Hardback
ISBN 0 521 63449 0 Paperback

Contents

Introduction	*page* vii
A Note on Editorial Method	xi
Editorial Symbols	xiii
Symbols Used to Describe Documents	xiv
Short Titles and Abbreviations	xv
Short Titles	xv
Abbreviations That Appear in the Documents	xvi
1 FREEDOM'S SOLDIERS: THE BLACK MILITARY EXPERIENCE	1
2 FREEDOM'S SOLDIERS: A DOCUMENTARY HISTORY	83
Illustrations between pages 50 and 82	
Sources of Documents	177
Suggestions for Further Reading	181
Index	185

Introduction

In the summer of 1862, the Sable Arm flexed its muscles as the first black men entered the Union army in parts of the occupied South. Their numbers were small, but, following the issuance of the Emancipation Proclamation on January 1, 1863, they were joined by free men of color who enlisted in specially commissioned Northern regiments. Then, beginning in May, with the establishment of the Bureau of Colored Troops, slaves flooded into the ranks. By war's end, some 179,000 black men had served in the Union army and another 18,000 in the navy.

The effect of black military service was electric—on friend and foe. The appearance of the Sable Arm shocked Confederate leaders, who denounced the enlistment of black soldiers as an invitation for slaves to rise against their owners. Jefferson Davis, the Confederate president, threatened to treat captured black soldiers not as prisoners of war but as slaves in insurrection—a threat all too often acted upon. Although the rebels' distress pleased white Northerners, many of them remained skeptical about the wisdom of arming black men. Gnawing doubts about the character of black people prompted even some committed opponents of slavery to question whether black men would, or could, fight.

Americans of African descent harbored no such doubts. Black men itched for the opportunity to liberate slaves and settle scores with slaveholders. As they moved onto the field of battle, black soldiers became heroes not only to their own people, but also to a war-weary

Northern populace. The military service of black men transformed the conflict between North and South from a war for the Union into a war for freedom. In the eyes of many, it proved decisive in securing a federal victory.

In the years that followed the war, the Sable Arm came to symbolize the triumph of the Union and the fulfillment of the founders' promise that all were created equal. Reminders of black military prowess opened the door to full political participation in the South and bent the colorline in the North. Confederate revanchists attested to the significance of black military service by their venomous assaults on former soldiers. For a generation, it seemed the nation would not forget.

But it did. Black veterans watched in dismay as the memory of their wartime heroics faded. During the last quarter of the nineteenth century, as the nation became preoccupied with sectional reconciliation, emancipation—and the role of black men and women in achieving it—became a source of embarrassment rather than pride. The triumph of segregation and disfranchisement further reduced black veterans in the eyes of most white Americans. By the early twentieth century, celebration of the Sable Arm had become lodged almost exclusively in the black community.

But just as changes in the political climate at the end of the nineteenth century obliterated the memory of black soldiers' role in the Civil War, so changes in the mid-twentieth century revived it. The Civil Rights movement, the participation of black soldiers in World War II, Korea, and especially Vietnam, and the achievements of black veterans, most notably General Colin Powell, awakened interest in freedom's soldiers.

In 1976, when the historians of the Freedmen and Southern Society Project began work on *Freedom: A Documentary History of Emancipation, 1861–1867,* the story of freedom's soldiers was high on their agenda. The project's first volume, *The Black Military Experience* (1982), provided rich evidence of the role of black soldiers, presenting several hundred letters—written by soldiers, their families, their officers, and other eyewitnesses—that described the soldiers' experiences, aspirations, and frustrations as they faced both treason and racism. Subsequent volumes of *Freedom,* especially *The Destruction of Slavery* (1985), added further evidence. Reviewers marveled at the power of the soldiers' story and the immediacy and eloquence of their words.

Since the publication of *The Black Military Experience,* scholarly and public interest in the Sable Arm has exploded. Some dozen scholarly volumes and articles on Civil War black soldiers have reached print, and others are on the way. In 1989 *Glory,* a cinematic rendition of the bloody assault on Fort Wagner by the 54th Massachusetts Infantry, appeared to rave reviews. Eight years later, the National Gallery of Art mounted an exhibition of the cast of Augustus Saint-Gaudens's frieze memorializing the soldiers of the 54th. Nearly every weekend, black men in blue uniforms with "U.S." on their brass buttons march, present arms, and perform military evolutions before interested spectators, black and white. Men, women, and young people search through crumbling pension files and service records to document their ancestors'—and their own—connection to the black soldiery. In the spring of 1998, a monument to African-American military service in the Civil War will be dedicated in the nation's capital. It will list the name of every black soldier in the Union army, as well as the white officers who led them.

Stirring and engaging though they may be, none of these memorials equals the force of the soldiers' own words and the words of those who observed their achievements. The commanding imagery of their language, often scribbled hastily and under duress, provides entry into the lives of black soldiers, their families, and their communities. In order to share those powerful words with a wider audience, the editors of *Freedom's Soldiers* have assembled this short and more accessible version of the soldiers' story from materials initially published in *The Black Military Experience* and other volumes of *Freedom.*

Like its parent volumes, *Freedom's Soldiers* is drawn from the records of the National Archives. It, too, rests on the work of the archivists and historians who have labored to preserve those records and make them accessible to the American people. Two deserve special mention. Sara Dunlap Jackson and Herbert G. Gutman, who shared a commitment to a broader understanding of the past, believed in this project when there was no project, and after it came into being, they helped protect it against budget cuts and administrative indifference.

Others have shared their vision. The University of Maryland has provided generous and continuous support to the Freedmen and Southern Society Project, as have two underfunded and underappreciated federal agencies, the National Historical Publications and Records Commission (NHPRC) and the National Endowment for the Humanities (NEH). The Freedmen and Southern Society Project would not have come into existence without the NHPRC, whose longstanding commitment to documentary publication has recently been placed in jeopardy by inadequate funding and resulting shifts in priorities. Nor could the Freedmen and Southern Society Project continue without support from the NEH, which of late has suffered grievously at the hands of congressional budget cutters.

If mighty institutions laid the foundations for *Freedom's Soldiers,* the labors of Terrie Hruzd, administrative assistant of the Freedmen and Southern Society Project, helped bring it to a successful conclusion. John P. Kaminski, himself the editor of a prominent documentary series, persuaded us that even a small book deserves an index, then proceeded to compile one of which we could be proud. And Frank Smith, our editor at Cambridge University Press, sped the volume into print so that it might join in celebrating the Union's black defenders.

A Note on Editorial Method

The editors have approached the question of transcription with the conviction that readability need not require extensive editorial intervention and, indeed, that modernization can compromise historical value. The body of each document in this volume is therefore reproduced exactly as it appears in the original—to the extent permitted by modern typography. All peculiarities of spelling, capitalization, punctuation, and syntax appear in the original. Illegible or obscured words that can be inferred with confidence are printed in ordinary roman type, enclosed in brackets. If the editors' reading is conjectural, a question mark is added.

Some adaptations are employed to designate characteristics of handwritten documents that cannot be exactly or economically reproduced on the printed page. Words underlined once in the manuscript appear in *italics*. Words underlined more than once are printed in SMALL CAPITALS. Interlineations are simply incorporated into the text at the point marked by the author. The beginning of a new paragraph is indicated by indentation, regardless of how the author set apart paragraphs.

The editors deviate from faithful reproduction of the body of each document in only two significant ways. First, the endings of unpunctuated or unconventionally punctuated sentences are marked with extra space. Second, some documents are not printed in their entirety, but each editorial omission is indicated by a four-dot ellipsis.

The editors intervene without notation in three minor ways.

When the author of a manuscript inadvertently repeated a word, the duplicate is silently omitted. Similarly, most crossed-out material is omitted without notation, since it usually represents false starts or ordinary slips of the pen. When, however, the editors judge that the crossed-out material reflects an important alteration of meaning, it is printed as ~~canceled type~~. In printed documents (only two of which occur in this volume), silent correction is made for jumbled letters and errant punctuation that appear to be typesetting errors. All other editorial interventions in the body of a document are clearly identified by being placed in italics and in brackets. These include descriptive interpolations such as [*In another handwriting*], the addition of words or letters omitted by the author, and the correction of misspelled words and erroneous dates. The editors exercise restraint in making such additions, however, intervening only when a document otherwise cannot be understood or is seriously misleading. In particular, no effort is made to correct misspelled personal and place names. When material added by the editors is conjectural, a question mark is placed within the brackets.

In the interest of saving space, the editors have adopted the following procedures for treating the peripheral parts of manuscripts. The inside and return addresses of a letter are omitted. (Instead, the text preceding each document conveys information about the sender and recipient, and the source citation supplies their names and titles exactly as they appear in the document.) The place and date are printed on a single line at the beginning of the document regardless of where they appear in the manuscript. The salutation and complimentary closing of a letter are run into the text regardless of their positions in the original. Multiple signatures are printed only when there are twelve or fewer names. For documents with more than twelve signatures, the editors indicate only the number of signatures on the signature line, for example, [*38 signatures*]. The formal legal apparatus accompanying documents such as sworn affidavits—including the names of witnesses and the name and position of the official who administered the oath—is omitted without notation.

Postscripts that concern matters unrelated to the body of a letter are similarly omitted.

A technical description symbol follows each document, usually on the same line as the signature. The symbol describes the physical form of the document, the handwriting, and the signature. (For a list of the symbols employed, see page xiv.)

Source citations for the documents published in *Freedom's Soldiers* are to the volumes of *Freedom: A Documentary History of Emancipation* where they were originally published and where full information may be found regarding their location in the National Archives.

EDITORIAL SYMBOLS

[roman] Words or letters in roman type within brackets represent editorial inference of parts of manuscripts that are illegible, obscured, or mutilated. A question mark indicates that the inference is conjectural.

~~canceled~~ Canceled type represents material written and then crossed out by the author of a manuscript. This device is used only when the editors judge that the crossed-out material reflects an important alteration of meaning. Ordinarily, canceled words are omitted without notation.

[*italic*] Words or letters in italic type within brackets represent material that has been inserted by the editors and is not part of the original manuscript. A question mark indicates that the insertion is a conjecture.

. . . . A four-dot ellipsis centered on a separate line represents editorial omission of a substantial body of material.

SYMBOLS USED TO DESCRIBE DOCUMENTS

Symbols describing the handwriting, form, and signature appear at the end of each document.

The first capital letter describes the handwriting of the document:

A   autograph (written in the author's hand)

H   handwritten by other than the author (for example, by a clerk)

P   printed

The second capital letter, with lower-case modifier when appropriate, describes the form of the document:

L	letter	c	copy
D	document	d	draft

The third capital letter (or its absence) describes the signature:

S   signed by the author

Sr   signed with a representation of the author's name

      no signature or representation

The more common symbols include ALS (autograph letter, signed by author), HLS (handwritten letter, signed by author), HLSr (handwritten letter, signed with a representation), HLcSr (handwritten copy of a letter, signed with a representation), HD (handwritten document, no signature).

Short Titles and Abbreviations

SHORT TITLES

Black Military Experience

    Freedom: A Documentary History of Emancipation, 1861–1867, series 2, *The Black Military Experience*, ed. Ira Berlin, Joseph P. Reidy, and Leslie S. Rowland (Cambridge, U.K., 1982).

Destruction of Slavery

    Freedom: A Documentary History of Emancipation, 1861–1867, series 1, volume 1, *The Destruction of Slavery*, ed. Ira Berlin, Barbara J. Fields, Thavolia Glymph, Joseph P. Reidy, and Leslie S. Rowland (Cambridge, U.K., 1985).

Official Records

    U.S. War Department, *The War of the Rebellion: A Compilation of the Official Records of the Union and Confederate Armies*, 128 vols. (Washington, 1880–1901).

Statutes at Large

    United States, *Statutes at Large, Treaties, and Proclamations of the United States of America*, 17 vols. (Boston, 1850–73).

Wartime Genesis: Lower South

    Freedom: A Documentary History of Emancipation, 1861–1867, series 1, volume 3, *The Wartime Genesis of Free Labor: The Lower South*, ed. Ira Berlin, Thavolia Glymph, Steven F. Miller, Joseph P. Reidy, Leslie S. Rowland, and Julie Saville (Cambridge, U.K., 1990).

Wartime Genesis: Upper South

    Freedom: A Documentary History of Emancipation, 1861–1867, series 1, volume 2, *The Wartime Genesis of Free Labor: The Upper South*, ed. Ira Berlin, Steven F. Miller, Joseph P. Reidy, and Leslie S. Rowland (Cambridge, U.K., 1993).

FREEDOM'S SOLDIERS

ABBREVIATIONS THAT APPEAR
IN THE DOCUMENTS

Asst.	Assistant
Brig., Brigr.	Brigadier
Capt.	Captain
Cav., Cav'y	Cavalry
Co.	Company
Col.	Colonel
comdg.	commanding
Dept.	Department
Dist.	District
do	ditto
Gen., Gen'l, Genl	General
Hd. Qrs.	Headquarters
Hon.	Honorable
Inf., Inft.	Infantry
inst.	*instant;* i.e., of the current month
Lt., Lieut.	Lieutenant
Maj., Majr.	Major
Obt. Servt., Obed^t Servt	Obedient Servant
Reg., Regt.	Regiment
Sergt., Sgt.	Sergeant
USCC, U.S.C. Cav.	U.S. Colored Cavalry
USCI, U.S.C. Inf.	U.S. Colored Infantry
USCT	U.S. Colored Troops
V., Vol., Vols.	Volunteers (usually preceded by a state abbreviation)
&c	et cetera

I

Freedom's Soldiers: The Black Military Experience

FREEDOM CAME to most American slaves only through force of arms. The growing Northern commitment to emancipation availed nothing without victory on the battlefield. But once federal policy makers had committed the Union to abolishing slavery, the Northern armies that eroded Confederate territory simultaneously expanded the domain of freedom. The Union army perforce became an army of liberation, and as it did, both the Northern public and the freed slaves themselves demanded that the direct beneficiaries of freedom join the battle against the slaveholders' rebellion. The incorporation of black soldiers into Union ranks at once turned to Northern advantage a vast source of manpower that the Confederacy proved incapable of tapping and enhanced the antislavery character of the war. The liberating force of black enlistments weakened slavery in the loyal border states and the Union-occupied South no less than in the Confederacy, thereby extending the nation's commitment to freedom beyond the limits of the Emancipation Proclamation. Black enlistees in the border states received their freedom, and, eventually, their enlistment also guaranteed the liberty of their immediate families. Throughout the slave states, black enlistment and slave emancipation advanced together and, indeed, became inseparable.

Black men coveted the liberator's role, but soldiering remained a complex, ambiguous experience. If most free blacks and slaves rushed to join the Union army, others entered federal service only at the point of a bayonet. Once enlisted, ex-slaves who yearned to confront their former masters on terms of equality found themselves enmeshed in another white-dominated hierarchy, which, like the one they had escaped, assumed their inferiority. Organized into separate black regiments, paid at a lower rate than white soldiers, denied the opportunity to become commissioned officers, often ill-used by commanders whose mode of discipline resembled that of slave masters, and frequently assigned to menial duties rather than combat, black soldiers learned forcefully of the continued inequities of American life. Nonetheless, the war left black soldiers with far more than their freedom. They gained new skills in regimental schools and a wider knowledge of the world in army service. Fighting and dying for the Union advanced the claims of black men and women to the rights and privileges of full citizenship. Victory over those who had previously dominated their lives bred a confidence that soldiers proudly carried into freedom and that permeated the entire black community. The successes of black soldiers in their war against discrimination within the army, however limited, politicized them and their families, preparing all black people for the larger struggle they would face at war's end.[1]

At the beginning of the war, few Union policy makers foresaw a military role for black men, free or slave. Southern leaders and Northern abolitionists may have placed slavery at the cornerstone of the Confederacy, but Northern policy makers minimized the connection between secession and chattel bondage. In the eyes of Northern leaders and most Northern whites, the conflict would be a war for Union—not against slavery—fought by the white men of

---

[1] This essay is based primarily upon documents published in the first four volumes of *Freedom: A Documentary History of Emancipation, 1861–1867* and other documents from the National Archives of the United States. For additional published primary sources and important secondary studies of black soldiers in the U.S. Civil War, see the suggested readings at the end of this volume.

Allen County Public Library
Saturday September 5 2015 01:01PM

Barcode: 31833037318257
Title: Freedom's soldiers : the Black...
Type: BOOK
Due date: 9/26/2015,23:59

Total items checked out: 1

Telephone Renewal:(260)421-1240
Website Renewal: www.acpl.info

each section. Most Union army commanders followed the same line of reasoning, even after local authorities in some parts of the South mustered a few free men of color into Native Guard units.[2] But as the Northern army confronted its enemy in the field, the indispensability of slavery to the Confederate war effort soon became evident. Southern armies depended heavily on the labor of slaves and free blacks to construct fortifications, transport materiel, tend cavalry horses, and perform camp services for both officers and enlisted men. Meanwhile, slaves on the home front raised the commercial staples necessary for foreign credit, labored in armories, shipyards, and ironworks to manufacture the weapons of war, and grew the food that fed both the army and the civilian population. Slave labor thus undergirded Confederate ability to wage war, while freeing Southern white men for battlefield service.[3] Indeed, as Union generals probed their adversary, they found that Confederate spokesmen had made no idle boast: Slavery stood at the center of Southern economy and society. The revelation gave new standing to abolitionists and their demand for emancipation. Slowly Union field commanders and then desk-bound policy makers came to see that preserving the Union required an assault upon chattel bondage.

General Benjamin F. Butler, a pugnacious politician with no previous military experience, first made the connection. Commanding the Union beachhead at Fortress Monroe in tidewater Virginia in the spring of 1861, Butler gave asylum to several runaway slaves, and, when their masters tried to reclaim the fugitive property, he

[2] On the free-black units, see *Black Military Experience*, docs. 11, 127; *Official Records*, ser. 4, vol. 1, pp. 1087–88, and vol. 2, pp. 197, 941; Mary F. Berry, "Negro Troops in Blue and Gray: The Louisiana Native Guards, 1861–1863," *Louisiana History* 8 (Spring 1967): 165–90; James G. Hollandsworth, Jr., *The Louisiana Native Guards: The Black Military Experience during the Civil War* (Baton Rouge, La., 1995), chap. 1; Charles H. Wesley, "The Employment of Negroes as Soldiers in the Confederate Army," *Journal of Negro History* 4 (July 1919): 239–53.

[3] On the Confederacy's dependence upon slave labor, see *Destruction of Slavery*, chap. 9; James H. Brewer, *The Confederate Negro: Virginia's Craftsmen and Military Laborers, 1861–1865* (Durham, N.C., 1969); Clarence L. Mohr, *On the Threshold of Freedom: Masters and Slaves in Civil War Georgia* (Athens, Ga., 1986), chap. 5; Ervin L. Jordan, Jr., *Black Confederates and Afro-Yankees in Civil War Virginia* (Charlottesville, Va., 1995), chap. 2.

sent the slaveholders packing. Initially, Butler acted out of an almost instinctive reluctance to aid the enemy. But, in a manner that came to characterize his command throughout the war, he quickly transformed his instincts into matters of high principle that flamboyantly redounded to his own and the North's benefit. Contending that slave property, like other private property, might rightfully be appropriated by the army upon grounds of military necessity, especially when such property was being employed in the enemy's cause, Butler put the fugitives to work in his quartermaster's department. Shall the rebels "be allowed the use of this property against the United States," Butler asked rhetorically, "and we not be allowed its use in aid of the United States?"[4] Thus Butler established a rationale for refusing to return fugitive slaves and for turning their labor to Union advantage, while at the same time evading the question of emancipation. Without challenging their status as property, pragmatic federal commanders could remove escaped or captured slaves from Confederate strength and add them to the Union side. The issue was captured property used by the enemy to wage war—"contraband of war"—not freedom.[5]

Northerners reveled in Butler's stroke, and the label "contrabands" adhered firmly to fugitive slaves. Other Union commanders hastened to follow Butler's lead. They increasingly perceived the value of black labor to their forces and also welcomed a solution to the problems posed by the escalating influx of fugitives into their lines. In August 1861, Congress—pressed by an upsurge in emancipationist sentiment in the North—gave legal standing to Butler's logic. The First Confiscation Act provided that a master who permitted his slave to labor in any Confederate service forfeited his claim to the slave.[6] However, as so often proved true during the war,

---

[4] *Destruction of Slavery,* docs. 1A–B.
[5] For the contraband-of-war argument as used by another Union commander, see *Destruction of Slavery,* doc. 42.
[6] *Statutes at Large,* vol. 12, p. 319.

events rapidly outran this legal position. With every advance of Union forces, slaves fled bondage and sought refuge with the Northern armies. With little regard for whether the fugitives had actually served the Confederacy, federal commanders turned the potential burden of civilian refugees into an asset by putting them to work on fortifications, on supply lines, and in personal service. Furthermore, as the war moved into its second year, support swelled for vigorous punishment of secessionists. Depriving rebels of their slaves appealed to Northerners frustrated by military stalemate and all too many defeats. Mindful of the apocalyptic vision of a vengeful God, some Northerners came to believe that their ultimate success hinged on elevating their struggle with the South to the level of high principle, demonstrating to themselves and to the world that they fought for right and justice and not for mere political or economic power. If the demands of the war sensitized Northerners to the moral necessity of freedom, the growing recognition of the evil of slavery awakened them to the South's dependence upon black laborers. Indeed, as the war dragged on, the various rationales for emancipation became increasingly detached from the motives of their advocates. Abolitionists touted the military advantages of emancipation, and generals denounced the immorality of slavery. The argument that each captured or fugitive slave put to work within federal lines would be, in effect, a net gain of two—one added to the Union, one lost to the Confederacy—grew in power. Increasing numbers of Northerners concluded that military as well as moral necessity demanded an end to slavery.[7]

Emancipation inched forward during the first half of 1862. Congress legislated compensated emancipation in the District of Columbia and prohibited slavery in the territories. President Abraham Lincoln—unsuccessfully—urged the slave states still in the

---

[7] On the development of federal policy and Northern public opinion concerning fugitive slaves, see *Destruction of Slavery*. On the employment of fugitive slaves as military laborers, see *Wartime Genesis: Upper South; Wartime Genesis: Lower South*.

Union to consider gradual, compensated emancipation.[8] Then, in July 1862, the Second Confiscation Act and the Militia Act formally adopted emancipation and the military employment of fugitive slaves as weapons of war. These acts declared "forever free" all captured and fugitive slaves owned by rebels and authorized the mobilization of "persons of African descent" in "any military or naval service for which they may be found competent."[9] If Lincoln's preliminary Emancipation Proclamation of September 1862 and the final proclamation of January 1, 1863, in effect freed no more slaves than had the Second Confiscation Act, they captured the imagination of the Northern public and elevated the Union's commitment to emancipation far beyond the level of mere expediency by adding moral weight to the Union cause. They also pledged the federal government to the full exploitation of black labor in defeating the Confederacy.[10]

Only a short step separated arguments about the value of black labor in support of the Union army and navy to proposals that black men be used even more directly against the Confederacy. The same military and moral necessity that enlarged Northern support for emancipation pushed the question of enlisting black soldiers to the fore, and, indeed, the two issues became increasingly intertwined.

[8] For the congressional legislation, see *Statutes at Large*, vol. 12, pp. 376–78, 432. On emancipation in the District of Columbia, see *Destruction of Slavery*, chap. 3. For the president's advocacy of gradual emancipation, see Abraham Lincoln, *Collected Works*, ed. Roy P. Basler, Marion D. Pratt, and Lloyd A. Dunlap, 9 vols. (New Brunswick, N.J., 1953–55), vol. 5, pp. 144–46, 160–61, 317–19, 324–25, 503–4, 529–34.

[9] *Statutes at Large*, vol. 12, pp. 589–92, 597–600.

[10] *Statutes at Large*, vol. 12, pp. 1267–69; John Hope Franklin, *The Emancipation Proclamation* (Garden City, N.Y., 1963). In theory the Emancipation Proclamation encompassed some slaves who were not entitled to freedom under the Second Confiscation Act, that is, slaves in the seceded states whose owners were loyal to the Union. In fact, however, most of the Confederacy's slaveholding unionists lived in regions that President Lincoln exempted from the proclamation because they were already under federal control and therefore no longer in rebellion. (The exempted areas were the state of Tennessee, the Virginia counties that became West Virginia, several counties in southeastern and northern Virginia, and the parishes of southern Louisiana.) The Second Confiscation Act freed slaves whose owners were disloyal to the Union, without geographical limitations; its provisions thus encompassed many slaves in the parts of the Confederacy exempted from the Emancipation Proclamation and in the border states, where the Emancipation Proclamation had no bearing.

Once emancipation found a place on the Union escutcheon, many white Northerners demanded that the blood of black men as well as white be shed to purchase the slaves' freedom, some for obviously self-serving motives, others believing that the participation of black people in the Union's victory would render the commitment to emancipation irreversible.[11]

Still, policy makers hesitated. The prospect of arming slaves or even free blacks raised fundamental questions about the place of black people in American society, questions that went far beyond the immediate demands of the war. After emancipating their slaves in the Revolutionary era, the Northern states had consigned them to the margins of society. White Northerners alternately exploited free-black men and women as cheap, menial laborers and urged their deportation from the United States, depriving them all the while of rights equated with freedom. Most Northern states denied black men the right to vote or to sit on juries, and several states prohibited black witnesses from testifying against whites. White Americans deemed bearing arms in defense of the Republic an essential element of citizenship, and federal legislation dating from 1792 restricted militia enrollment to white men.[12] As recently as 1859, Massachusetts Governor Nathaniel P. Banks had vetoed a law that would have incorporated black men into the state forces.[13] Black people and their abolitionist allies challenged these proscriptions as denials of both the fundamental rights of man and the rights of citizens, and they protested racial discrimination. Thus, enlisting black men into the Union army not only would suggest a measure of equality most Northerners refused to concede, but also

[11] For examples of various arguments, see *Wartime Genesis: Lower South,* docs. 159–60; *Black Military Experience,* docs. 21, 24–25.

[12] Leon F. Litwack, *North of Slavery: The Negro in the Free States, 1790–1860* (Chicago, 1961).

[13] Francis W. Bird, *Review of Governor Banks' Veto of the Revised Code, on Account of Its Authorizing the Enrollment of Colored Citizens in the Militia* (Boston, 1860); Elon A. Woodward, comp., "The Negro in the Military Service of the United States, 1639–1886," pp. 946–50, Colored Troops Division, Adjutant General's Office, National Archives.

would enlarge the claims of black people to full citizenship. For these reasons, black enlistment raised questions few Northern leaders willingly confronted. Both Congress and the Lincoln administration moved cautiously.

If Union policy makers dreaded the implications of black enlistment, black Northerners and other abolitionists welcomed them. From the beginning of the war, Northern black men pressed for the opportunity to serve in the army.[14] They were joined by abolitionists, free-soilers, and a few career military officers of antislavery persuasion who also saw black enlistment as a lever against slavery and racial discrimination. Governor John A. Andrew of Massachusetts stood at the front of this group. Conscious of both the vital need for manpower and the ideological implications of arming black men, in 1862 he began peppering the War Department with requests for permission to raise a free-black regiment within his state's volunteer organization. Simultaneously, James H. Lane, veteran of the Kansas border wars and now a U.S. senator from that state, pressed for and eventually assumed similar authority.[15] Two career army officers also lent early support to black enlistment: General John W. Phelps, a Vermont abolitionist serving in the Department of the Gulf, and General David Hunter, commander of Union forces along the coast of South Carolina, Georgia, and Florida. Although the military command structure circumscribed Phelps and Hunter in ways that hardly affected Andrew or Lane, the strategic positions of the two generals and their explicit advocacy of slave—as well as free-black—recruitment strengthened the bond between enlistment and emancipation.

In the summer of 1862, Phelps and Hunter, acting independently and on their own authority, armed fugitive-slave men and pressed for War Department recognition of their troops. Both soon ran afoul

[14] See, for example, *Black Military Experience*, docs. 17–23; Dudley Taylor Cornish, *The Sable Arm: Negro Troops in the Union Army, 1861–1865* (New York, 1956), pp. 1–7; James M. McPherson, *The Negro's Civil War: How American Negroes Felt and Acted during the War for the Union* (New York, 1965), chap. 2.
[15] On Andrew, see *Black Military Experience*, pp. 75–76, and doc. 26. On Lane, see *Black Military Experience*, pp. 44–45, and docs. 12–15; Cornish, *Sable Arm*, chap. 4.

of their superiors. Phelps tangled with Butler—now in command of the Department of the Gulf—and was quickly mastered by the practiced politician. Hunter, who also barged ahead without War Department approval, had to disband his slave regiment when it failed to receive official sanction and thus could be neither uniformed nor paid. But, although Phelps and Hunter received public reprimands and reversals, events moved so quickly that their previously unacceptable policies soon won official blessing. Butler, after forcing Phelps's resignation, not only armed black men—free rather than slave—but also shamelessly claimed credit for initiating black enlistment. Similarly, within weeks of the dissolution of Hunter's regiment, Secretary of War Edwin M. Stanton authorized Hunter's subordinate, General Rufus Saxton, to raise several regiments among contrabands on the South Carolina sea islands.[16]

Yet the War Department's expectations in sanctioning the employment of black soldiers were different from those of Phelps or Hunter. The two generals had hoped to field a slave army of liberation; the department saw the enlistment of black men as a stopgap measure to ease manpower shortages in a few military theaters. The War Department neither proposed large-scale black enlistment nor connected black enlistment to the emerging national emancipation policy. But, if federal policy makers were not yet fully committed to a black soldiery, the organization of a few black regiments in Louisiana, South Carolina, and Kansas provided early opportunities for black men to demonstrate their eagerness to enlist and their potential as soldiers, important precedents upon which the proponents of enlistment could draw.

Military setbacks in the summer and fall of 1862 reoriented

16 On Phelps's recruitment, see *Black Military Experience*, pp. 41–44, and docs. 9–10. On his conflict with Butler, which involved differences regarding emancipation policy as well as recruitment, see also *Destruction of Slavery*, pp. 192–96, and docs. 59, 61–63, 67A; Cornish, *Sable Arm*, pp. 56–65. On the recruitment of Hunter's regiment and its effects, see *Wartime Genesis: Lower South*, docs. 20–21; *Black Military Experience*, pp. 37–41, and docs. 1–4; Cornish, *Sable Arm*, pp. 33–55. For the order authorizing Saxton to enlist black men, see *Wartime Genesis: Lower South*, doc. 36.

Union priorities. Just as military necessity prompted Congress and President Lincoln to make emancipation the centerpiece of federal war policy, so the course of the war eroded the obstacles to full-scale enlistment of black men. Differences between the preliminary Emancipation Proclamation of September 1862 and the final proclamation of January 1863 suggest changes in Lincoln's thinking even over the brief three-month period. Whereas the former made no mention of arming emancipated slaves, the latter expressed an intention to receive slaves freed by the proclamation into military service to garrison forts and other military installations.[17] After the new year, Secretary of War Stanton also showed greater awareness of the military advantages of arming large numbers of contrabands, as well as the need to find employment for the thousands of fugitives thronging army camps. In March 1863, he created the American Freedmen's Inquiry Commission to investigate the condition of refugee slaves and report "what measures will best contribute to their protection and improvement, so that they may defend and support themselves; and also, how they can be most usefully employed in the service of the Government for the suppression of the rebellion."[18] Thus, by early 1863 the Lincoln administration had tied the question of slavery to the larger issues of the nature of the war, the impact of emancipation on American society, and the role of black people in the war effort. These issues could not easily be separated, and the insatiable demand for soldiers forced the question of black enlistment to the fore. The previously inconceivable idea of large-scale enlistment of black men appeared increasingly to be common sense.

Union manpower needs gave new leverage to the proponents of enlistment. Protracted warfare overwhelmed the War Department's initial plan to supplement the small regular army with a volunteer

[17] *Statutes at Large,* vol. 12, pp. 1267–69. The final proclamation also declared that slaves emancipated by its provisions would be received into armed service on navy vessels. Congress had laid the legal foundations for black military service in the Second Confiscation Act and the Militia Act.

[18] *Official Records,* ser. 3, vol. 3, p. 73. For the commission's reports, see *Official Records,* ser. 3, vol. 3, pp. 430–54, and ser. 3, vol. 4, pp. 289–382.

force. Men who had entered the army enthusiastically under Lincoln's early calls for volunteers, and who had reenlisted for additional terms of service, grew impatient with the bloody stalemate, as families suffered during their absence and the death toll mounted. The number of new volunteers plummeted, worsening the army's already serious manpower shortage. Scrambling to fill depleted Union ranks, Congress in March 1863 required systematic enrollment of all male citizens aged twenty through forty-five and provided for conscription by lottery from the enrollment lists.[19] The legislation flouted popular opposition, forced military service upon the unwilling, and fueled resistance to both the draft and the war itself. The increasing manpower demands inexorably shifted Northern perceptions of the utility of enlisting black men, especially when combined with the belief that, since black people would clearly benefit from Union victory, white soldiers should not bear the entire burden of battle. The white potential draftee looked with increasing favor upon the idea of filling Union ranks with black men, even if he cared little about emancipation or disdained black people altogether. And the same manpower needs that compelled Congress to draft white men hastened a War Department commitment to enlist black men.[20]

With Governor Andrew and others pressing the case and with black regiments already established in Louisiana, in South Carolina, and—under something less than official sanction—in Kansas, the Lincoln administration slowly, grudgingly, but irrevocably, turned

[19] *Statutes at Large*, vol. 12, pp. 731–37. On the enrollment and conscription system and popular resistance to it, see James W. Geary, *We Need Men: The Union Draft in the Civil War* (DeKalb, Ill., 1991); Eugene Converse Murdock, *Patriotism Limited, 1862–1865: The Civil War Draft and the Bounty System* (Kent, Ohio, 1967), and *One Million Men: The Civil War Draft in the North* (Madison, Wisc., 1971); Fred A. Shannon, *The Organization and Administration of the Union Army, 1861–1863* (Cleveland, Ohio, 1928), vol. 1, pp. 295–323, and vol. 2, pp. 11–243. See also Grace Palladino, *Another Civil War: Labor, Capital, and the State in the Anthracite Regions of Pennsylvania, 1840–68* (Urbana, Ill., 1990), chap. 5.

[20] On the connection between the draft and growing support for black enlistment, see *Wartime Genesis: Upper South*, doc. 223; *Black Military Experience*, docs. 29–30, 33–34, 76, 100.

to black men to offset the shortage of white soldiers. Early in 1863, Secretary of War Stanton authorized the governors of Rhode Island, Massachusetts, and Connecticut to organize black regiments. But, as if to emphasize the tentative nature of the commitment, he balked when Ohio Governor David Tod asked for similar authority. Black volunteers from Ohio and the other Northern states would have to enlist in the New England regiments.[21]

Stanton's restriction scarcely hindered the abolitionists. Before long, Andrew and others had commissioned antislavery radical George L. Stearns to recruit black men throughout the free states. Stearns, in turn, organized citizens' committees, raised money, and hired black recruiting agents to scour the North. With long years of experience in the abolition movement and deep roots in Northern black communities, men like Martin R. Delany, O. S. B. Wall, John Mercer Langston, and John Jones had no trouble locating recruits and forwarding them to the regimental rendezvous in New England.[22] Their efforts benefited from the public support of nearly all Northern black leaders. In July, a convention of black men from across the state of New York resolved that the disease of rebellion "having proved to be incurable by ordinary means, such as Reason, Justice, [and] Patriotism . . . [,] more effective remedies ought now to be *thoroughly* tried, in the shape of warm lead and cold steel, duly administered by two hundred thousand black doctors."[23] That same summer, as the Massachusetts, Rhode Island, and Connecticut regiments filled, Stanton authorized other Northern governors to initiate black recruitment in their own states. Since black volunteers counted toward state draft quotas, most of the governors happily complied.[24]

---

[21] *Black Military Experience*, pp. 75–76, and docs. 28, 31–33, 38A.

[22] *Black Military Experience*, docs. 30–32, 34–37, 142, 144; Cornish, *Sable Arm*, pp. 106–11.

[23] *Record of Action of the Convention Held at Poughkeepsie, N.Y., July 15th and 16th, 1863, for the Purpose of Facilitating the Introduction of Colored Troops into the Service of the United States* (New York, 1863). Quotation on p. 8.

[24] *Black Military Experience*, docs. 33–35. The grudging compliance of the Democratic governor of New York, Horatio Seymour, was an exception to the rule. (*Black Military Experience*, docs. 38A–C.)

While authorizing the enlistment of free-black men in the North, Stanton also moved to expand recruitment of slave men in the Union-occupied South. He dispatched General Daniel Ullmann to southern Louisiana, assigned General Edward A. Wild to North Carolina, and sent Adjutant General Lorenzo Thomas to the Mississippi Valley to give slave enlistments full official sanction. Stanton charged Ullmann with raising a black brigade in the Gulf region, a task for which Ullmann had been preparing in New York since the new year. Pushed by Massachusetts Governor Andrew, Stanton authorized Wild to inaugurate recruitment in the Union's tidewater North Carolina foothold, and he headed south to organize what became known as Wild's African Brigade. As befitted his rank, Thomas shouldered weightier responsibilities. In addition to raising black troops, he would coordinate contraband policy with the Treasury Department and convince white soldiers of the virtues of black enlistment.[25]

Adjutant General Thomas's appointment, embodying a shift from haphazard recruitment of black men by interested parties and independent commanders to a systematic, centrally coordinated recruitment policy, confirmed the change in the War Department's approach. Thomas found skeptics aplenty within the commands of Generals Ulysses S. Grant and William T. Sherman; Sherman, among others, would never be fully convinced.[26] But the Union had made a commitment to arming black men, and growing manpower demands only deepened it. In May 1863, the War Department established the Bureau of Colored Troops to regulate and supervise the enlistment of black soldiers and the selection of officers to command black regiments.[27] From the spring of 1863 to the end of the

[25] On the extension of recruitment to the occupied South, see *Black Military Experience*, chap. 3. On Adjutant General Thomas's activities, see *Destruction of Slavery*, doc. 110; *Wartime Genesis: Lower South*, chap. 3; *Black Military Experience*, docs. 62, 194; Cornish, *Sable Arm*, chap. 7.
[26] For examples of hostility to black enlistment on the part of federal military officers, see *Black Military Experience*, docs. 39B, 50–51.
[27] *Official Records*, ser. 3, vol. 3, pp. 215–16.

war, the federal government labored consistently to maximize the number of black soldiers.

During the summer of 1863, events at home and on the battlefield enlarged the government's commitment to the recruitment of black men. On the war front, Northern military victories at Gettysburg and Vicksburg arrested the Confederate offensive in the North and divided the Confederacy. The Union army's southward march—especially in the Mississippi Valley—stretched supply lines, brought thousands of defenseless ex-slaves under Union protection, and exposed large expanses of occupied territory to Confederate raiders, further multiplying the army's demand for soldiers. On the home front, these new demands sparked violent opposition to federal manpower policies. The Enrollment Act of March 1863 allowed wealthy conscripts to buy their way out of military service by either paying a $300 commutation fee or employing a substitute. Others received hardship exemptions as specified in the act, though political influence rather than genuine need too often determined an applicant's success. Those without money or political influence found the draft especially burdensome.[28] In July, hundreds of New Yorkers, many of them Irish immigrants, angered by the inequities of the draft, lashed out at the most visible and vulnerable symbols of the war: their black neighbors.[29] The riot raised serious questions about the enrollment system and sent Northern politicians scurrying for an alternative to conscription. To even the most politically naive Northerners, the enlistment of black men provided a means to defuse draft resistance at a time when the federal army's need for soldiers was increasing. At the same time, well-publicized battle achievements by black regiments at Port Hudson and Milliken's Bend, Louisiana, and at Fort Wagner, South Carolina, eased popular

[28] See above, note 19.
[29] Iver Bernstein, *The New York City Draft Riots: Their Significance for American Society and Politics in the Age of the Civil War* (New York, 1990), especially pt. 1; Adrian Cook, *The Armies of the Streets: The New York Draft Riots of 1863* (Lexington, Ky., 1974).

fears that black men could not fight, mitigated white opposition within army ranks, and stoked the enthusiasm of both recruiters and black volunteers.

However firm, official commitment to black enlistment did not of itself put black men into uniform. In the Northern free states, where recruiters had full access to the black population, the number of potential recruits was small. According to an estimate by the superintendent of the census, only 46,000 black men of military age resided in those states (see Table 1), so that Northern free blacks alone could not hope to meet the Union's manpower requirements. The largest number of black men within reach of army recruiters resided in the border slave states that had remained in the Union (Maryland, Delaware, Missouri, and Kentucky) and in those parts of the Confederate states occupied by federal forces before the end of 1862 (especially Tennessee and southern Louisiana). But in these areas, which were unaffected by the Emancipation Proclamation or specifically exempted from it, white unionists—many of them slaveholders—raised powerful objections to the recruitment of black men. Fearful for their property, they alternately threatened to desert the Union and claimed unflinching devotion to it in order to prevent the enlistment of slaves, or even free blacks.[30] At first Union policy makers respected such claims, especially while Confederate forces still contended for military control of the states in question. But although the Lincoln administration sought to avoid alienating loyal masters, many of whom carried considerable political weight, it still desperately desired to tap these vast reserves of potential soldiers.

In each border state, and in Tennessee and Louisiana as well, the administration weighed the value of slaveholder unionism against the army's manpower needs. The reading of the scale varied from place to place and time to time depending upon the course of the

[30] For examples of objections by unionists, see *Destruction of Slavery*, doc. 168; *Black Military Experience*, docs. 75, 84, 97–98. On the border states, see *Black Military Experience*, chap. 4.

TABLE I
Black Soldiers in the Union Army and Black Male Population
of Military Age in 1860, by State

State	Black male population, ages 18 to 45			Black soldiers	
	Free	Slave	Total	Number credited to the state	Percentage of black men ages 18 to 45
Northern free states					
Maine	272	–	272	104	
New Hampshire	103	–	103	125	
Vermont	140	–	140	120	
Massachusetts	1,973	–	1,973	3,966	
Connecticut	1,760	–	1,760	1,764	
Rhode Island	809	–	809	1,837	
New York	10,208	–	10,208	4,125	
New Jersey	4,866	–	4,866	1,185	
Pennsylvania	10,844	–	10,844	8,612	
District of Columbia[a]	1,823	–	1,823	3,269	
Ohio	7,161	–	7,161	5,092	
Indiana	2,219	–	2,219	1,537	
Illinois	1,622	–	1,622	1,811	
Michigan	1,622	–	1,622	1,387	
Wisconsin	292	–	292	165	
Minnesota	61	–	61	104	
Iowa	249	–	249	440	
Kansas	126	–	126	2,080	
Subtotal				37,723	
Black soldiers recruited in Confederate states but credited to Northern free states[b]				(5,052)	
Total	46,150	–	46,150	32,671	71
Union slave states					
Delaware	3,597	289	3,886	954	25
Maryland	15,149	16,108	31,257	8,718	28
Missouri	701	20,466	21,167	8,344	39
Kentucky	1,650	40,285	41,935	23,703	57
Total	21,097	77,148	98,245	41,719	42

| | Black male population, ages 18 to 45 | | | Black soldiers | |
| | | | | Number credited to the state | Percentage of black men ages 18 to 45 |
State	Free	Slave	Total		
Confederate slave states					
Virginia	9,309	92,119	101,428	5,919[c]	6
North Carolina	5,150	55,020	60,170	5,035	8
South Carolina	1,522	70,798	72,320	5,462	8
Florida	131	12,028	12,159	1,044	9
Georgia	583	83,819	84,402	3,486	4
Alabama	391	83,945	84,336	4,969	6
Mississippi	130	85,777	85,907	17,869	21
Louisiana	3,205	75,548	78,753	24,052	31
Texas	62	36,140	36,202	47	<1
Arkansas	22	23,088	23,110	5,526	24
Tennessee	1,162	50,047	51,209	20,133	39
Subtotal				93,542	
Black soldiers recruited in Confederate states but credited to Northern free states[b]				5,052	
Total	21,667	668,329	689,996	98,594	14
Other areas	2,041[d]	–	2,041	5,991[e]	
Total for all areas	90,955	745,477	836,432	178,975	21

Note: The percentage of each state's black military-age population that entered the army is merely an approximation; fugitive slaves frequently enlisted in regiments outside their home states (the number of black soldiers credited to Kansas and the District of Columbia, for example, was notably swelled by such enlistments), and other population movements make the 1860 census figures somewhat inadequate for comparison with enlistment statistics. Because the early Massachusetts, Connecticut, and Rhode Island black regiments recruited throughout the North, state-by-state computation of population percentages for the free states would be misleading; hence, only a regional percentage is given.

[a] Congress had already ended slavery in the District of Columbia at the time these population figures were compiled.

[b] Enlisted under the act of July 4, 1864, that permitted Northern state agents to recruit black men in the Confederate states. See *Official Records*, ser. 3, vol. 5, p. 662.

[c] Virginia, 5,723; West Virginia, 196.

[d] California, 1,918; Oregon, 38; Colorado, 5; Nebraska, 15; Nevada, 27; New Mexico, 16; Utah, 5; Washington, 17.

[e] Colorado Territory, 95; state or territory unknown, 5,896.

Source: Population figures come from a report by the superintendent of the census, based upon the 1860 census (see *Black Military Experience*, doc. 27); the number of black soldiers credited to each state is given in the 1865 report of the Bureau of Colored Troops (*Official Records*, ser. 3, vol. 5, p. 138).

war, the nature of white unionism, and the viability of slavery. But everywhere slaves, fleeing to Union lines to offer military service in exchange for freedom, shifted the balance against their owners. Often they did so at considerable risk, for many "loyal" slaveholders would rather have seen their slaves in a shroud than in a uniform. Everywhere slaveholders tried to discourage enlistment by threatening to abuse or sell the families of black volunteers, and then, when that strategy failed, frequently made good the threats.[31] The willingness of slaves to venture all for freedom intertwined the politics of enlistment with the politics of emancipation, and, when military necessity triumphed over political expediency, enlistment effected black freedom in those areas of the South untouched by the liberating provisions of the Emancipation Proclamation.

Military need for laborers also confounded the recruitment of black soldiers. Quartermasters and engineers increasingly depended on black teamsters, dockhands, and laborers to supply Union forces and construct fortifications. The opportunity to remain near family and friends and, frequently, to earn higher and more regular pay made such employment more attractive than uniformed service to many black men. Thus, as the number of available black men shrank, competition between quartermasters and recruiters intensified. Although the War Department resolved the problem differently at different times, this competition shaped black enlistment throughout the war.[32]

As early as the beginning of 1864, enlistment had so undermined slavery in some places that slaveholders who wished to retain a labor

[31] On measures taken to deter border-state black men from enlisting and to punish the families of those who nevertheless did so, see *Destruction of Slavery*, docs. 146, 188, 190–93, 231, 233, 235, 237; *Wartime Genesis: Upper South*, docs. 181, 225A–C, 226, 229; *Black Military Experience*, docs. 74, 88, 90–94, 100–101, 103, 105–7, 294, 296–98, 302–4, 312B.

[32] On federal employment of black military laborers, see *Wartime Genesis: Upper South*; *Wartime Genesis: Lower South*. On the government's "competing with itself" for the labor of black men, see *Wartime Genesis: Upper South*, docs. 217n., 223; *Black Military Experience*, docs. 45–46.

force were often compelled to acknowledge the freedom of their slaves in practice, if not in principle. To prevent slave men from running away and joining the Union army, they offered wages and other accouterments of freedom.[33] In such cases, freedom lost its power as an incentive for enlistment, and the slaves' enthusiasm for military service waned. Moreover, as the war dragged on, black men, like white, learned that military service entailed considerable suffering, not only for themselves but also for their families. Many who had managed to carve out freedom and earn a living outside the army saw little reason to enlist. When the stream of black volunteers slowed, the army frequently resorted to impressment. Press gangs—sometimes composed of black soldiers—rode roughshod over potential recruits, and conscription often became indistinguishable from kidnapping. Wartime freedom thus acquainted black people with new forms of compulsion.[34]

Black men resisted impressment as they had resisted slavery and often forced Union commanders to modify coercive recruitment practices. Federal policy makers searched for more legitimate means to fill depleted military ranks. In February 1864, Congress revised the much-abused Enrollment Act, eliminating many of its inequities and also making all black men in the Union states— slaves included—subject to the formal procedures of enrollment and conscription.[35] The revised Enrollment Act threatened white Northerners with a draft that could no longer be evaded by paying a commutation fee, even as substitutes were becoming increasingly difficult and expensive to obtain. Citizens' committees and local and state governments offered new and larger bounties to volunteers— white or black—who would fill draft quotas. The Northern states

[33] See, for example, *Wartime Genesis: Upper South*, docs. 105, 107, 125, 188, 222; *Black Military Experience*, doc. 96.

[34] On the impressment of black soldiers, see *Wartime Genesis: Upper South*, docs. 75, 79, 106B, 129; *Wartime Genesis: Lower South*, docs. 57, 163, 165, 193; *Black Military Experience*, docs. 6A–B, 47A–C, 52–54C, 56–58, 81–82, 84, 170A–B.

[35] *Statutes at Large*, vol. 13, pp. 6–11.

also sought permission to recruit black men in the Confederate states, counting such recruits toward Northern state quotas and paying them sizable bounties. Congress complied in July 1864, and Northern agents spread across the Union-occupied South, indiscriminately enlisting and impressing black men. Many of the new recruits were already in Union employ, and their enlistment infuriated military employers and their superiors.[36] In March 1865, Congress repealed the enabling legislation,[37] but the problem of impressment remained, and abusive conscription continued to the end of the war.

By the spring of 1865, voluntary enlistment and conscription had placed 179,000 black men in the Union army, forming, together with the black men who served in the navy, 10 percent of those who served in the Northern armed forces.[38] Of this number, approximately 33,000 enlisted in the free states. The border states of Delaware, Maryland, Missouri, and Kentucky accounted for a total of nearly 42,000, more than half from Kentucky. Tennessee contributed 20,000; Louisiana, 24,000; Mississippi, nearly 18,000; and

[36] For one Northern request to recruit black men in the South, see *Black Military Experience*, doc. 39A. For the legislation authorizing such recruitment, see *Statutes at Large*, vol. 13, pp. 379–80; on recruitment under its provisions, see *Black Military Experience*, pp. 76–78, and doc. 39B.

[37] *Statutes at Large*, vol. 13, p. 491.

[38] Although it is impossible to determine precisely the number of black sailors in the Union navy, research by Joseph Reidy and graduate students at Howard University suggests a figure of approximately 18,000 men and several dozen women. Their investigation, which is supported by the Department of the Navy and the National Park Service, has attempted to examine every type of extant personnel record for references to persons of African ancestry. The resulting total is substantially higher than that of 9,596 offered by David L. Valuska on the basis of reports from designated enlistment depots. (*The African American in the Union Navy: 1861–1865* [New York, 1993], pp. 82–83.) It is also substantially lower than the conjecture by naval officials that black men accounted for 25 percent of navy enlistments or 29,511 total, upon which estimate a number of historians have relied. (See Herbert Aptheker, "The Negro in the Union Navy," *Journal of Negro History* 32 [Apr. 1947]: 169–200.) For a preliminary description of the Howard University project, see Joseph P. Reidy, "Black Jack: African American Sailors in the Civil War Navy," in *New Interpretations in Naval History: Selected Papers from the Twelfth Naval History Symposium Held at the United States Naval Academy, 26–27 October 1995,* ed. William B. Cogar (Annapolis, Md., 1997), pp. 213–20.

the remaining states of the Confederacy accounted for approximately 37,000 (see Table 1).

The participation of black men in the Union army varied from place to place. In some areas nearly every man of military age served, in others hardly any. Everywhere freedom provided the most powerful stimulus to enlistment. In the border states, where slavery remained legal through most of the war (and, in Kentucky and Delaware, even after it ended), a large proportion of black men joined the army. Missouri's share of the Union's black soldiers, for example, was nearly twice the state's proportion of the nation's black men, even without counting fugitive slaves from Missouri who joined the army in neighboring Kansas. In Kentucky, where, beginning in early March 1865, slave volunteers could free not only themselves but also their families,[39] army service claimed nearly three-fifths of the black men of military age. Only 5 percent of the nation's black men resided in Kentucky at the start of the Civil War, and many had fled to enlist in Northern and Tennessee regiments before recruitment was finally permitted in their home state, yet the black soldiers credited to Kentucky constituted more than 13 percent of the total. However, in areas where the Union army arrived late in the war and freedom derived from the Emancipation Proclamation, few black men enlisted. Although Alabama and Georgia together contained 20 percent of all black men aged eighteen to forty-five, only 5 percent of all black troops enlisted from those states. In Texas, where federal operations began even later

---

[39] On March 3, 1865, by joint resolution, Congress provided for the freedom of the wives and children of all men serving in, or subsequently mustered into, army or navy service. (*Statutes at Large*, vol. 13, p. 571.) For instances of soldiers' relatives claiming freedom under the resolution, see *Destruction of Slavery*, docs. 239, 243; *Wartime Genesis: Upper South*, docs. 222, 237, 240–41; *Black Military Experience*, docs. 110, 112. The Militia Act of July 1862 had declared "forever free" the mothers, wives, and children of black men who had belonged to disloyal masters and then rendered service to the United States, but only if the family members were also owned by disloyal masters—a qualification that excluded the families of most border-state black soldiers. (*Statutes at Large*, vol. 12, p. 599.) Both Maryland and Missouri abolished slavery by state action before the March 1865 joint resolution.

and involved only a small part of the state, a token forty-seven black soldiers saw Union service, from a population of more than 36,000 black men of military age. This variety in the black military experience affected the struggle for freedom both during the war and in the years that followed.

Enlistment not only strengthened the bondsman's claim to freedom; it also enhanced the freeman's claim to equality. As free blacks and their abolitionist allies had argued from the beginning of the war, Northern black men welcomed the chance to strike at slavery as a means of acquiring all the rights of citizens. Although the figures do not allow precise calculation, it appears that in many areas of the North proportionately more black men served in the Union army than white men. The Census Office estimated in 1863 that fewer than 10,000 black soldiers would be obtained from the free states if black men enlisted in the same proportion as white men had; yet more than three times that number served in Northern black regiments, an impressive showing even after discounting for the enlistment of some Southern fugitives and Canadian émigrés in the Northern units.[40]

As the North debated the question of enlisting black men in the Union army, a similar discussion took shape in the Southern states. Measured by letters and memorials to the Confederate Secretary of War and other Southern officials, it followed the outline of the Northern debate. Like white Northerners, white Southerners— many of them slaveholders—argued that a "nigger" could stop a bullet as well as a white man; black enlistment would save white lives. Confident of the loyalty of their slaves, some slave owners itched to array slave men against the arrogant Yankees and thus authenticate the South's beneficent view of slavery. Others initially recoiled from the prospect of arming slaves, but their reluctance diminished once the North began recruiting black men. An enemy that stooped to such barbarism, they argued, deserved retaliation in

[40] See *Black Military Experience,* doc. 27, for the Census Office estimate.

kind. As in the North, wartime necessity added urgency to these arguments, and the call for slave enlistment grew more insistent as Confederate military fortunes deteriorated.

Yet in some important respects, the Southern debate differed sharply from the Northern one. Only a handful of free people of color and virtually no slaves pleaded for a chance to fight for Southern nationality and black bondage. Moreover, the South's decision to arm slaves lagged well behind the North's. Whereas Union officials accepted some slave soldiers in 1862 and began large-scale recruitment in early 1863, Confederate authorities inaugurated slave enlistment only in the desperate spring of 1865, when the war was already lost. Northern and Southern understandings of the implications of black armed service contrasted most dramatically in the combatants' respective positions about enlisting slaves and enlisting free blacks. Although the South countenanced free-black military service long before the North contemplated such a move, the Confederate government's reluctance to interfere with slavery prohibited Southern consideration of arming slaves until long after the North could expediently do so and, indeed, until the whole question had become moot.[41]

Once enlisted, black soldiers had much in common with Billy Yank or even Johnny Reb. They experienced the same desperate loneliness of men fearful for their lives and separated from family and friends. The same reveille blasted them from their bunks in the morning, and the same tattoo put them to bed at night; the same mosquitoes invaded their tents in the summer, and the same wind whistled through their barracks in the winter. Like white soldiers, they enlisted expecting the glory of great battles but often found themselves wielding shovels rather than rifles. They too grumbled about

---

[41] On the Confederate debate over enlisting black soldiers, see *Black Military Experience,* chap. 5; Robert F. Durden, *The Gray and the Black: The Confederate Debate on Emancipation* (Baton Rouge, La., 1972). On those few free-black soldiers who served the Confederacy early in the war, see the sources cited above, in note 2.

long hours on the drillfield, complained about overbearing officers, and bemoaned the quality of army rations. And, like soldiers everywhere, they found relief in the camaraderie of the campfire.[42]

Yet, if military life created countless similarities, the seemingly insoluble distinctions between slave and free, black and white nevertheless remained. A white Northern private might boast of fighting for the Union and $13 a month, just as a Southern one might claim he battled for Bobby Lee and his homeland, but few black soldiers could see the war in such narrow terms. Many owed their liberty to military enlistment, and most understood that the freedom of all black people depended upon Union victory. Across the field, behind the hedge, Johnny Reb might spy a money-grubbing Yankee, just as Billy Yank might see a sotted aristocrat, but black soldiers confronted men who had sold their parents, put their sisters in the field, and scarred them with the lash, and who would gladly clap them back into bondage. Knowledge that their own freedom and that of their posterity hung in the balance made black soldiers Union patriots.[43]

The timing and circumstance of their enlistment deepened the black soldiers' commitment to the Union and magnified their expectations about the rewards of military service. Entering the war at the Union's ebb, black soldiers came to believe that they had shifted the balance from the Confederate to the Union side. In return, they hoped that their participation would infuse federal emancipation policy with a commitment to equality. Whereas many

[42] On the motivations and experiences of common soldiers during the Civil War, see Bell Irvin Wiley, *The Life of Billy Yank: The Common Soldier of the Union* (Indianapolis, Ind., 1951), and *The Life of Johnny Reb: The Common Soldier of the Confederacy* (Indianapolis, Ind., 1943); James I. Robertson, Jr., *Soldiers Blue and Gray* (Columbia, S.C., 1988); Reid Mitchell, *Civil War Soldiers* (New York, 1988), and *The Vacant Chair: The Northern Soldier Leaves Home* (New York, 1993); James M. McPherson, *What They Fought For, 1861–1865* (Baton Rouge, La., 1994), and *For Cause and Comrades: Why Men Fought in the Civil War* (New York, 1997). On the soldiers in battle, see Gerald F. Linderman, *Embattled Courage: The Experience of Combat in the American Civil War* (New York, 1987); Earl J. Hess, *The Union Soldier in Battle: Enduring the Ordeal of Combat* (Lawrence, Kans., 1997). On camp life among black soldiers, see *Black Military Experience,* chap. 13.
[43] See, for example, *Black Military Experience,* docs. 22, 54D, 207, 218, 299A–B, 300–301.

contemporaries—Southern as well as Northern—shared this understanding of the importance of the entry of black soldiers into the war, only a handful of white Northerners believed that black military service implied a commitment to equality, and then, perhaps, only equality before the law. So if black men celebrated their acceptance into the ranks as a sign of a dramatic alteration of their place in American society, they soon learned that the changes they envisioned came slowly if at all. In fact, instead of speeding black people down the road to equality, federal officials frequently formulated policies that confirmed the established pattern of invidious racial distinctions.

Union policies at all levels shaped the distinctive nature of the black military experience. Many of them sprang effortlessly from the historical legacy of slavery and discrimination. For example, although a few light-skinned black men passed silently into white regiments,[44] no one ever gave serious consideration to placing white and black soldiers in the same units.[45] More commonly, federal policy respecting black soldiers evolved slowly and painfully against the backdrop of the war's changing fortunes, congressional and administrative politics, and Northern popular opinion. Whatever

---

[44] One such free-black soldier was Private Charles R. Pratt, a member of the 11th Ohio Infantry. In August 1864, while stationed near Atlanta, Pratt applied for transfer to the black 55th Massachusetts Infantry on the following grounds: "I am a colored man, and my position as private in a white Regiment is very unpleasant. My feelings are constantly outraged by the conduct of those who have no respect for my race." A company commander in another Ohio white regiment, also stationed near Atlanta, petitioned in September 1864 for the transfer of four men of mixed racial origins ("one of them very dark") from his company to an Ohio black regiment. While assuring the Secretary of War that he favored the use of black troops, he contended that "the presence of these men cause great dissatisfaction among the white soldiers and occasion myself a great deal of trouble to keep order and quiet in the company and is I think an injustice both to myself and the men to have them where they now are." The War Department readily complied with both requests. (Priv. Charles R. Pratt to Brig. Genl. L. Thomas, 3 Aug. 1864, P-276 1864, and Lieut. Henry C. Reppert to Hon. E. M. Stanton, 17 Sept. 1864, R-314 1864, both in Letters Received, ser. 360, Colored Troops Division, Records of the Adjutant General's Office, RG 94, National Archives.)

[45] In the Union navy, by contrast, black sailors served on the same ships with white sailors, probably as a result of longstanding seafaring custom. Like their counterparts in the army, however, black sailors filled the lowest ranks. (See Valuska, *African American in the Union Navy,* chap. 5.)

their origin, these policies touched all aspects of the lives of black soldiers, from their diet to their duties, from their relations with their officers to their relations with their families. But two Union policies proved particularly significant in giving form to the black military experience: excluding black men from commissioned office and paying black soldiers less than their white counterparts. While not necessarily more blatant in intent or effect than other discriminatory actions, these two policies fully revealed the racial inequities of federal military service. They provoked massive protests by black soldiers and their abolitionist allies and captured the attention of the general public. The questions of commissions and pay thus not only set black soldiers apart from white ones, but also encouraged black soldiers to make common cause among themselves. Although they wore the same uniform as white soldiers, observed the same articles of war, answered to the same system of military justice, and confronted the same enemy, black soldiers fought a different war. Because they struggled to end inequality as well as to save the Union, they faced enemies on two fronts, battling against the blue as well as the gray to achieve freedom and equality.

When black soldiers first entered the Union army, the assurances of federal officials—from Secretary of War Stanton to local recruiters—that those who fought under the American flag would enjoy its full protection and benefits blinded all but the most prescient to the question of treatment after enlistment.[46] Thus, the first black soldiers recruited in the sea islands of South Carolina and the sugar parishes of Louisiana expected to be treated like other soldiers, and at first it appeared they would be. The appointment of black officers did not appear to be an issue in the sea islands, where General David Hunter organized the first slave regiment, but the free colored Louisiana Native Guard units, mustered into service by General Benjamin F.

---

[46] For assurances of equal treatment and protection, see *Wartime Genesis: Lower South,* doc. 57; *Black Military Experience,* docs. 28, 31, 37, 148, 151, 154, 156A–C, 157B, 158A, 158D, 158F, 159–60D, 161, 202, 291. For examples of early doubts of black Northerners about equal treatment within the army, see *The Christian Recorder,* 26 July 1862, 14 Feb. 1863.

Butler, served from the start under officers of their own color. These black officers, almost all free by birth, worldly, and well-educated, had so impressed Butler that he readily offered them commissions in Union ranks. Recognizing the close bonds between the officers and the enlisted men, and anticipating the importance of black commissioned officers for future Union recruitment, Butler also organized a second Louisiana Native Guard regiment, with many black officers selected from men of the first regiment, and had begun recruiting a third, consisting partly of escaped slaves as well as free men of color, when his tenure as department commander ended late in 1862. As manpower shortages and the impressive performance of the Native Guard dispelled Butler's initial skepticism about the military aptitude of black men, his confidence in the ability of black officers grew.[47]

However, Butler's successor, General Nathaniel P. Banks, considered the black officers unfit for command and determined to eliminate them from the service and replace them with white men. Banks devised a variety of stratagems, ranging from formal boards of examination to outright deception, to purge the black commissioned officers. Though a few remained in the three Louisiana Native Guard regiments until mid-1864, Banks's action confirmed War Department skepticism about the advisability of commissioning black officers.[48]

Black Northerners and antislavery proponents of black enlistment like Governor Andrew in Massachusetts and Senator Lane in Kansas also assumed that commissioned offices would follow logically upon the admission of black men to armed service. During the summer of 1862, Lane had gone so far as to sign commissions for several black recruiters of his 1st Kansas Colored Volunteers. The War Department, however, silently refused to recognize their validity, reducing

[47] *Black Military Experience,* p. 305, and doc. 127; Manoj K. Joshi and Joseph P. Reidy, "'To Come Forward and Aid in Putting Down This Unholy Rebellion': The Officers of Louisiana's Free Black Native Guard during the Civil War Era," *Southern Studies* 21 (Fall 1982): 326–42; Hollandsworth, *Louisiana Native Guards,* chaps. 2–3. On black officers more generally, see *Black Military Experience,* chap. 6.

[48] *Black Military Experience,* pp. 305–7, and docs. 128–32; Hollandsworth, *Louisiana Native Guards,* chaps. 4, 7.

Lane's commissions to a hollow promise. Skeptical of the ability of black men to lead and fearful of the reaction of white soldiers to the appointment of black men to superior office, Secretary of War Stanton refused to commission black line officers throughout 1863 and 1864. During this period, black men attained commissioned office only as chaplains and surgeons—positions with the rank of major but outside the chain of command. Even these appointments came grudgingly and were accompanied by a hail of abusive complaints from white officers and enlisted men.[49]

Black people vehemently protested the War Department's exclusionary policies. The free colored former officers of the Louisiana Native Guard spearheaded the protest. They were soon joined by Northern free blacks and their white allies, who believed the appointment of black officers would give talented black men an opportunity to demonstrate the full capabilities of their race.[50] Soldiers in the 54th and 55th Massachusetts Infantry regiments pressed both their officers and Governor Andrew for promotion, and early in 1864 Andrew tested the War Department's determination to exclude black officers. Exercising a governor's authority over troops raised in his state, Andrew offered a lieutenancy to Sergeant Stephen A. Swails, an educated, light-skinned freeman who had compiled an exemplary military record. When the War Department blocked Andrew's action, Swails and others barraged federal authorities with demands for a favorable ruling. As the protest mounted, the battlefield valor of black soldiers, especially noncommissioned officers, steadily eroded the department's position. The combined pressure of black soldiers and Northern abolitionists weakened the opposition to black officers. When a long list of prominent Republican politicians added their approval early in 1865, the War Department

[49] On Andrew and Lane, see *Black Military Experience,* pp. 44–45, 304–5, and docs. 14–15, 134–36, 161. On black chaplains and surgeons, see *Black Military Experience,* pp. 309–10, and docs. 144–47; Edwin S. Redkey, "Black Chaplains in the Union Army," *Civil War History* 33 (Dec. 1987): 331–50.
[50] *Black Military Experience,* docs. 129–32, 134A–B, 139–40.

agreed to commission Swails.[51] Yet, even with the end of the war in sight, the department resisted wholesale appointment of black officers and succeeded in confining their number to a mere handful and restricting their service to a few—mostly Northern—regiments. Indeed, most black officers received their commissions after the cessation of hostilities and served as officers only briefly before their regiments were mustered out.[52]

The pay they received also distinguished black soldiers from their white counterparts.[53] Believing the assurances of the early army recruiters and recruitment broadsides, black enlistees assumed that they would receive the same remuneration as white soldiers. But the War Department ruled that the legal basis for black military service lay in the 1862 Militia Act and paid all black soldiers according to its provisions: $10 per month, minus $3 for clothing, rather than the $13 per month, plus clothing, that white privates received. Even black commissioned and noncommissioned officers received the same $7 monthly pay, so that the highest-ranking black officer earned barely half the compensation of the lowest-ranking white enlisted man.[54]

Unequal pay angered black soldiers as perhaps no other Union policy did. The reduced income imposed a severe strain on families dependent upon black soldiers for their support, but the principle mattered at least as much. Black men in the army, those recruiting soldiers, and those contemplating enlistment, as well as their advocates in the antislavery movement, attacked the discriminatory pay policy as yet another vestige of second-class citizenship. Led by black soldiers recruited in the free states and encouraged by sympathetic

---

[51] *Black Military Experience*, docs. 141A–C.

[52] *Black Military Experience*, pp. 308, 310–12.

[53] On federal pay policies and the struggle of black soldiers for equal pay, see *Black Military Experience*, chap. 7, and docs. 199, 202; Herman Belz, "Law, Politics, and Race in the Struggle for Equal Pay during the Civil War," *Civil War History* 22 (Sept. 1976): 197–222; Cornish, *Sable Arm*, pp. 181–96; McPherson, *Negro's Civil War*, chap. 14.

[54] For the pay provisions of the Militia Act, see *Statutes at Large*, vol. 12, p. 599. For the pay allotted white soldiers of various ranks, see U.S. War Department, *Revised United States Army Regulations* (Washington, 1863), pp. 358–63.

white officers, several regiments refused to accept the $7 monthly pittance, regarding it as an affront to their dignity as American soldiers. Rather than submit to inferior treatment some went more than a year without pay. The 54th and 55th Massachusetts regiments even refused Governor Andrew's offer to use state funds to increase their compensation to the amount white privates received. In the meantime, they fought and died, dug fortifications and fell ill, and fumed at the progressive impoverishment of their families.[55] In late 1863, the protest boiled over in open revolt. Black soldiers in the 3rd South Carolina Infantry, led by Sergeant William Walker, stacked their arms and refused to perform duty until the army granted equal pay. Walker's superiors charged him with mutiny and executed him as an example to other black protesters.[56] But Walker's death did not stem the protest. Instead, black soldiers stationed in other parts of the South began to agitate for change. Many teetered on the brink of mutiny until Congress passed an act equalizing the pay of black and white soldiers in June 1864.[57]

The War Department's inability to sustain its guarantees of equal treatment provoked no less fury than its overtly discriminatory practices. Confederate refusal to accord captured black soldiers the rights due prisoners of war demanded that Union policy makers ensure black soldiers the protection of the flag. Although numerous Union commanders, from regimental officers to President Lincoln, declared their readiness to retaliate in kind if the Confederates acted on their threat to hang or enslave black prisoners, enforcing federal policy proved difficult. Even the most unambiguous evidence—such as the Confederate slaughter of black soldiers after the surrender of Fort Pillow, Tennessee—never seemed proof enough for most Union officials. The reluctance, if not refusal, of federal officers to make good their promise of retaliation meant that black soldiers faced dangers white ones seldom encountered. This special vulnera-

---

[55] *Black Military Experience*, pp. 364–67, and docs. 153–58A, 159–60.
[56] *Black Military Experience*, docs. 158A–F.
[57] For the law, see *Statutes at Large*, vol. 13, pp. 129–30.

bility of black soldiers marked another distinctive aspect of the black military experience. Knowing that death or enslavement might follow capture, they fought all the more desperately for the Union. Knowing that the federal government offered them less protection than their white comrades, they remained alienated from the Union for which they fought and pressed for equal protection.[58]

Other distinguishing features of black military life arose from neither explicit policy decisions nor their haphazard enforcement but from the unspoken assumptions of American race relations. Dealings between black soldiers and their officers generally followed the familiar pattern of white superiors and black subordinates and thus carried all the historic burdens of white-black relationships in the United States. But the diverse expectations both black soldiers and white officers brought to soldiering complicated the traditional pattern of American race relations still further. As committed abolitionists, some white officers volunteered to lead black troops as a means of demolishing racial stereotypes and fulfilling their own egalitarian vision. Glorying in the epithet "nigger officers," they befriended their men and promoted their cause. Other white officers accepted positions in black regiments only in quest of rapid advancement. They cared nothing for the cause of freedom or racial equality and despised their men all the more because of the stigma attached to serving with black soldiers.[59]

Few white officers of black regiments exhibited all the characteristics of either the abolitionist or the careerist; instead they combined attitudes derived from the two seemingly contradictory positions. At each extreme, white officers exercised command in a variety of ways. Moreover, since black soldiers responded to their officers with similar diversity, the relationship between white officers and black soldiers

[58] On black prisoners of war, see *Black Military Experience*, chap. 12; Cornish, *Sable Arm*, chap. 9. On the Fort Pillow massacre, see *Black Military Experience*, docs. 214A–C; John Cimprich and Robert C. Mainfort, Jr., eds., "Fort Pillow Revisited: New Evidence about an Old Controversy," *Civil War History* 28 (Dec. 1982): 293–306.

[59] On the white officers of black regiments, see *Black Military Experience*, chap. 8; Cornish, *Sable Arm*, chap. 11; Joseph T. Glatthaar, *Forged in Battle: The Civil War Alliance of Black Soldiers and White Officers* (New York, 1990), especially chaps. 2–3.

defies easy categorization. If some black soldiers found support and comfort serving under men of antislavery conviction, others found the well-meaning paternalism of abolitionist officers more distasteful than the simple contempt of racist commanders. Black soldiers resented being treated like children no less than being treated like chattel. But whatever the specific pattern of relationships, the fact that the line of command within black regiments generally coincided with the color line added still another distinguishing element to black military life.[60]

The complex pattern of Union policies, their irregular enforcement, and the unspoken assumptions that stood behind them touched all aspects of black military life. In addition to influencing relations between enlisted men and their officers, the treatment they could expect if captured, the pay they received, and their prospects for promotion from the ranks, federal policies affected the nature of military justice and discipline, the care afforded sick and wounded soldiers, and the food, clothing, and equipment issued to healthy ones. Taken together, the policies of the federal government sensitized black soldiers to any act that might be deemed discriminatory. In such a context, racially innocent actions inexorably acquired racial meaning. The harsh discipline white officers meted out to black subordinates may in many instances have differed little from their punishment of white inferiors. In the eyes of former slaves, however, a white man striking or publicly humiliating a black man conveyed an unambiguous image of slavery. Just as white officers instituted policies based upon their understanding of racial differences, black soldiers protested perceived abuses.[61]

The timing of their entry into the Union army, like their antebellum experience and their subjection to discriminatory Union poli-

---

[60] On relations between black soldiers and their officers, see *Black Military Experience,* chaps. 8–9, and docs. 176, 178, 181–83, 187, 199, 240; Glatthaar, *Forged in Battle,* especially chaps. 4–6.

[61] On military discipline and punishment, see *Black Military Experience,* chap. 9, and docs. 336, 341; Glatthaar, *Forged in Battle,* chap. 6.

cies, guaranteed that black soldiers would view the war differently than white soldiers. By the middle of 1863, when a significant number of black troops took the field for the first time, white soldiers had been battling the rebels for more than two years. Many of them had grown disenchanted with a war that seemed to have no end, and a considerable number evinced little sympathy for changing Union war aims—particularly emancipation. Black soldiers rarely shared this estrangement, however disillusioned they might have been by some aspects of federal policy. Having struggled for the right to bear arms in defense of their country, they were eager to strike a blow against the slaveholding South. Whereas many white soldiers wearied as the war dragged on, the enthusiasm of black soldiers grew with the Union's commitment to freedom and to the effort—however feeble and reluctant—to eliminate the most glaring racial inequities from military life.

The timing of their entry into the army affected black soldiers in other ways as well. The war made different demands on Union soldiers after 1863 than before. By the time black soldiers took the field, Confederate forces had been swept from the Mississippi Valley and parts of the Atlantic seaboard. With their removal, the Union army required large bodies of troops to secure the vast expanse of the occupied South and to protect its lengthening supply lines. No matter who composed the federal army after 1863, thousands of Union soldiers would be guarding railroad bridges and telegraph lines, manning artillery stations, constructing fortifications, and protecting contraband camps. That black men entered the war just at the moment Union manpower needs took a new form determined much of the course of black military service.

Could they fight? The question haunted the debate over black enlistment and followed black soldiers into the army. Black soldiers longed for the opportunity to test their mettle on the field of battle and thus resolve lingering doubts about their manhood and demonstrate their worthiness for full citizenship. However, the Union army needed large numbers of soldiers to do everything but fight. That need complemented the widespread belief that black men could handle shovels better than guns and that, as the Emancipation Proclamation suggested, black soldiers should serve mainly to relieve white ones for front-line duty. In many instances, black soldiers found themselves serving as nothing more than uniformed laborers.[62]

Heavy fatigue duty wore out clothing as quickly as it wore down bodies. When black soldiers exhausted their $3 monthly clothing allowance, quartermasters deducted the cost of additional clothing from their $7 monthly pay, thus salting the wound of discriminatory pay. Long days of fatigue duty strung end to end sapped the morale of black soldiers, and insufficient drill compromised their military efficiency. Both they and their officers, including many antislavery champions of black enlistment, protested discriminatory labor assignments that neither military strategy nor the dignity of Union service seemed to warrant. But if they protested, they could lift but an enfeebled voice in search of public sympathy, and if black soldiers threatened mutiny, they were often too tired even to stack their arms, let alone raise them. Finally, in the face of overwhelming evidence of injustice, the most damning of which was the disproportionately high morbidity afflicting black soldiers, in June 1864 Adjutant General Thomas banned excessive fatigue duty for black troops and required that their assignments to labor details be proportionate to those of their white comrades. Many commanders ignored the order and continued to work black soldiers more like beasts of burden than national defenders, but eventually General Thomas's order established a norm.[63]

---

[62] On black soldiers and fatigue duty, see *Black Military Experience,* chap. 10. See also *Wartime Genesis: Upper South,* docs. 100, 218, 223, 230; *Black Military Experience,* docs. 62, 154, 265, 294, 314E.

[63] For protests by black soldiers and their officers against excessive and disproportionate fatigue duty, see *Black Military Experience,* docs. 198–200, 202, 204–5B, 205D–E, 206. For Thomas's order, see *Black Military Experience,* doc. 201.

Just as Union policies and the course of the war distinguished the lives of black soldiers from those of white ones, so they fractured the black military experience in a variety of ways. Black soldiers brought diverse experiences and expectations to soldiering. Some had grown up in cities, attended schools taught by prominent clergymen, traveled widely, and enjoyed freedom for generations. Others had come from the insular, tightly circumscribed world of the plantation and knew little of life beyond the slave quarter. Some entered military service as young men, hardly more than children; others joined the army late in life and had children of their own. Whether black soldiers had been free men or slaves, Northerners or Southerners, artisans or field hands, whether they had been raised among the black majority of the Carolina lowcountry or the white majority of the Northern states—all these circumstances in some measure influenced the course of black military life. Such diversity shaped the reactions of black soldiers to Union policies and affected their implementation. Free blacks, who were generally better educated and more cosmopolitan than slaves, marched into military service with different hopes and aspirations. Although black soldiers who had just escaped bondage may well have seen military service as payment for their freedom—as many Union officials suggested— those who had been free before the war saw little personal gain in the reward of liberty. The inequities of black military life thus seemed particularly galling to those black soldiers who had been free. Not surprisingly, they led demands for commissioned office and monopolized those ranks after Union policy changed. Brandishing a protest tradition generations in the making and mobilizing their connections with white antislavery advocates, they initiated complaints about federal pay policies and other inequities within the army. Although soldiers who had been slaves joined these protests and initiated still others, the free-black regiments generally took the lead. However, regiments composed of former slaves appear to have resorted to direct action—Sergeant Walker's mutiny, for example—more often than did the former freemen, perhaps because former slaves enjoyed less complete mastery of the mechanism of formal petitioning or less confidence in its efficacy.

Differences among black soldiers extended beyond the mechanics of protest to the sources of grievance. Lack of sensitivity to distinctions among black men frequently left white officers mystified at the variety of reactions to the same policies. When commissary officers altered the diet of black soldiers to include more pork and corn bread, Southern-born soldiers welcomed the change, but their Northern-born comrades, accustomed to beef and wheat bread, complained bitterly.[64] In ways similar if not as dramatic, cultural differences between those who practiced skilled trades and enjoyed literacy and those who lacked skills or education affected the deployment of black soldiers and their relations with their officers and their fellow soldiers. Even within slave regiments, artisans, house servants, and other privileged bondsmen provided the bulk of the noncommissioned officers. The structure of the black community shaped the structure of black military life. Occasionally, physiological differences supplemented cultural ones. Like white men, black men raised in different disease environments had developed different immunities, so that for some black soldiers assignment to subtropical regions confirmed commonplace stereotypes about the ability of black people to survive in such areas, whereas for others it inevitably spelled disaster.[65]

Although the changing nature of the war consigned many black soldiers to labor and support duties, it sent others into fierce confrontations with the enemy. Again, the time and place of enlistment, the skills and knowledge black men brought to soldiering, the personal temperament and political influence of particular commanders, and the Union army's need for front-line troops all helped determine

---

[64] *Black Military Experience*, docs. 263, 267, 273.

[65] On the health of black soldiers, see *Black Military Experience*, chap. 15, and doc. 205F. See also Paul E. Steiner, *Medical History of a Civil War Regiment: Disease in the Sixty-Fifth United States Colored Infantry* (Clayton, Mo., 1977).

who would fight and how they would fight. From the moment black soldiers entered the war, politically potent abolitionist proponents of black enlistment pressed the War Department and army field officers to send black soldiers against the enemy to demonstrate that black men could and would stand up to the master class. At Port Hudson, Milliken's Bend, and Fort Wagner, black soldiers quickly proved that battlefield heroics knew no color line. But even after they had established their martial credentials, black soldiers did not all enjoy the same opportunity to confront Confederate forces. Because of their earlier entry into the war and their abolitionist connections, units composed disproportionately of Louisiana and Northern freemen played a large role in the early battles, as did the first slave soldiers recruited in South Carolina and Louisiana. In the years that followed, the considerable reputations of these first regiments, as well as their strategic locations, continued to thrust them into combat. Other black regiments, organized later and in different political and military circumstances, rarely engaged the enemy. In the Mississippi Valley, for example, most black soldiers saw little fighting, in some measure because Union troops had already secured the region but also because many of the region's commanders remained skeptical of the military abilities of black men.

Nonetheless, the changing course of the war could deprive even skeptical commanders of the luxury of excluding black men from battle and could put black soldiers face to face with the enemy. In the final grueling operations of the eastern theater, General Ulysses S. Grant summoned every available Union soldier to assault the Confederate strongholds in Virginia. Grant's armies included the largest concentration of black troops engaged at any time during the war, most of them eventually organized into the Union army's only all-black army corps. In the trenches before Richmond and Petersburg, black soldiers, like white ones, dug earthworks, held the Union lines, pressed the rebel defenses, and at long last participated in the triumphant march into the capital of the vanquished Confederacy. Thus by war's end nearly all black soldiers had received a taste of combat, though even then the course of the war continued to determine how they fought.[66]

For the men who fought, the Civil War was a momentous event that molded their lives and those of their descendants in countless ways. It elevated some to new heights of glory and power, propelling them into political and entrepreneurial careers. It shattered others. The thousands of limbless men found in all corners of America long after the shooting stopped provided grim reminders of the war's continuing impact. For generations after the war ended, the outcome of the struggle determined the social relations, economic standing, and political allegiance of millions of Americans. That emancipation accompanied enlistment for most black soldiers heightened the impact of military service on black life. Because so many black soldiers simultaneously achieved freedom and reached maturity, the military experience took on an even larger meaning for the men, their families, their communities, and, ultimately, the entire society.

Soldiering provided black men with more than legal freedom. In dramatic and undeniable ways military service countered the degradation that had undermined black self-esteem during the antebellum years. Battlefield confrontations with the slaveholding enemy exhilarated black soldiers by demonstrating in the most elemental manner the essential equality of men. But nothing more fully reveals the revolutionary impact of soldiering on black life than the transit of black men from slaves to liberators. In smashing the manacles that bound their people, black soldiers elevated themselves and transformed their own consciousness. In their own eyes, in the eyes of the black community, and, however reluctantly, in the eyes of the

---

[66] On the combat experience of black soldiers, see *Black Military Experience,* chap. 11, and docs. 163, 276B; Cornish, *Sable Arm,* chaps. 8, 13, and pp. 240–43, 258–60; Glatthaar, *Forged in Battle,* chaps. 7–8.

nation, black men gained a new standing by donning the Union blue and participating in the nation's great triumph.[67]

A good deal of the liberating force of the black military experience derived not from monumental battles or stark confrontation with bondage but from military routine. Black soldiers savored the dignity of standing picket, with the power to challenge all trespassers, whatever their race or rank. As participants in foraging parties, they witnessed the futile anger of former masters who lost their slaves, their crops, their livestock, and even their homes to the claims of "military necessity." They gained a new sense of their own place in society while guarding captured Confederate soldiers, whose dejected demeanor and powerless situation contrasted markedly with former boasts of racial superiority and military invincibility. Even the most mundane activities—the mastery of the manual of arms, the deployment of large, complicated weapons, and the execution of complex evolutions—provided new sources of pride and accomplishment.

Beyond the battlefield and the drillfield, military service transformed the lives of black soldiers. As slaves or even freemen, black men had generally viewed the world through a narrow lens. As soldiers, they traveled broadly, met a wider variety of people, and expanded their range of experience. More important, black soldiers had occasion to see the world from positions of dominance as well as subordination. Although they continued to answer to higher authority, black soldiers frequently found themselves in circumstances in which they alone commanded the field. Their new knowledge and authority burst the bonds of subservience bred by slavery and second-class citizenship. Soldiering thus granted black men far greater control over their own destiny and fostered a new self-confidence.

Skills and knowledge gained in military service enlarged this new self-confidence. Army schools offered black soldiers access to the

[67] On the postbellum significance of wartime military service, see *Black Military Experience,* chaps. 17–18; *Destruction of Slavery,* doc. 244.

printed word, an opportunity legally denied slaves and even some black freemen before the war. Black soldiers, like freedpeople generally, rushed to take advantage of book learning. Literacy not only allowed black soldiers to communicate with their families and advance into the noncommissioned ranks, but also provided the means to petition against injustice and to articulate their vision of the new world of freedom. Education in the army advanced along other lines as well. Regimental chaplains tutored black soldiers in a variety of subjects, practical as well as moral. Although many chaplains filtered their message through a brand of religious paternalism that the soldiers found unpalatable, lectures on everything from sanitary procedures to the Constitution of the United States enlarged the world of men long kept ignorant of such subjects and encouraged them to widen their intellectual horizons. In many regiments, black soldiers joined together to build schools, hire teachers, and form literary and debating societies.[68]

The struggle for equality within the Union army also taught important lessons. Not only did congressional provision of equal pay and the War Department's tardy acquiescence on the question of commissioning black officers stir optimism about eventual equality, but the struggle itself awakened men previously excluded from the political process to the possibilities of redressing their grievances, informed them of the means by which their goals might be achieved, and identified the federal government as a forum for obtaining justice. Northern free blacks had a long tradition of political protest, and they drew on it freely. But the tactics pioneered by Northern freemen passed quickly to slave soldiers, most of whom had no formal political experience. Before long, regiments composed of newly liberated slaves petitioned and protested with all the skill and tenacity of those whose members were freeborn, demanding that the gov-

---

[68] *Black Military Experience,* chap. 14, and docs. 145A, 169, 274, 334, 342; John W. Blassingame, "The Union Army as an Educational Institution for Negroes, 1862–1865," *Journal of Negro Education* 34 (Spring 1965): 152–59; Dudley Taylor Cornish, "The Union Army as a School for Negroes," *Journal of Negro History* 37 (Oct. 1952): 368–82.

ernment they fought to preserve accord them and their families the dignity and protection due all its citizens. In so doing, former slaves learned something about the system of government under which Americans lived. They came to understand that justice depended not on the favor of a single powerful individual, but on impersonal rules and regulations that governed all citizens. Even though some army officers played the petty tyrant and others willingly countenanced such autocratic behavior, behind their arbitrary actions stood a forest of regulations that ruled military life. In learning how to deal with abstract law as well as personal authority, previously enslaved black soldiers took their first steps as free men. And in the process, they not only asserted their claim to citizenship, but also broke down the barriers that distinguished freemen and bondsmen and thereby unified the black community as never before.[69]

Military service also offered some black soldiers opportunities for advancement that far exceeded those available during the antebellum years. Although the War Department balked at commissioning black officers until late in the war, it had no objection to the appointment of black men to the noncommissioned ranks. Indeed, the difficulties inherent in balancing the often antagonistic interests of officers and enlisted men in a highly charged racial atmosphere encouraged Union officials to turn this task over to selected black soldiers. Standing between the largely white officer corps and the black privates, black sergeants and corporals played a role similar to that of a factory foreman or even an antebellum slave driver. Although they enjoyed a considerable measure of power, their authority was never large enough to satisfy either those below or those above them in rank. Their responsibilities for assignment and discipline frequently alienated black enlisted men without gaining the approbation of white officers. But because black noncommissioned officers camped with the other enlisted men and shared their daily routine, as well as so many other common experiences, they

---

[69] On black soldiers' experience with military law and justice, see *Black Military Experience,* chap. 9.

generally gained the trust of the men they led. Black soldiers frequently took their problems and grievances to their sergeants and corporals, who in turn presented them to higher authorities. Advocacy of this kind exacted a toll, as rebuffs brought reduction in rank or other punishments. But black noncommissioned officers—along with the few commissioned ones—generally gained in stature from their wartime service and transferred their positions of leadership to civilian life when the war ended.[70]

The black military experience affected many black people who never wore the Union uniform. From the moment of enlistment, military service altered the lives of black soldiers' families. In some places, enlistment ensured their safety and secured their freedom. In the border states, where slavery was unimpeached by the Emancipation Proclamation, the enlistment of husbands and fathers established the only claim to liberty for many soldiers' families. Elsewhere, black soldiers guarded contraband camps and Union-held plantations to prevent Confederate raiders from recapturing and reenslaving loved ones. But the same act of enlistment that provided protection for some black families encouraged the abuse and confinement of others. Angry masters who vowed to take revenge upon women and children whose husbands, sons, and fathers dared to enlist had little compunction about making good their threats.[71]

After enlistment, the experience of black soldiers continued to shape the lives of those who remained behind. The questions of equal pay and protection, which appeared in the guise of abstract justice to interested white people, touched the wives and children of black soldiers in a direct and immediate manner. After all, the treat-

[70] For examples of black noncommissioned officers serving as advocates for lower-ranking enlisted men, see *Black Military Experience*, docs. 153–54, 157A, 158C–D, 175, 180, 189, 190A, 248, 268.

[71] On black soldiers' families, see in particular *Black Military Experience*, chap. 16. For claims to freedom based upon the enlistment of husbands, sons, and fathers, see, for example, *Destruction of Slavery*, docs. 239, 243; *Wartime Genesis: Upper South*, docs. 222, 237, 240–41; *Black Military Experience*, docs. 110, 112. On the abuse of family members, see the sources cited above, in note 31.

ment accorded black prisoners was a matter of life and death, and the difference between $7 and $13 per month was the difference between subsistence and starvation for many black families. By the same token, the impoverished condition of families left at home or liable to abuse by Confederate guerrillas or former masters influenced the conduct of black soldiers. Nothing more surely moved them to protest than news of the material hardship or physical suffering of their families.[72]

Because black men served as soldiers and black women did not, military service created important differences in the way they experienced the war and emancipation. Army life exposed black men to the rigors of the march and the perils of battle, but it also incorporated them into an institution whose power and sovereignty dramatically superseded that of the slaveholders. When black women met the slaveholding enemy, they only occasionally did so under direct military auspices—as, for example, when General Edward A. Wild handed three slave women a whip and invited them to settle scores with their master. If armed service, in all its various aspects, helped liberate black men from the narrow confines of bondage and second-class citizenship, black women enjoyed no comparable experience. Whatever changes the war brought to women's lives, they rarely equaled the dramatic elevation in status that accompanied military duty. At the heart of that elevated status, moreover, lay a portrayal of black men as the liberators and defenders of their people. One recruitment order particularly solicited "[m]en of family" because, in protecting contraband camps, "they will, as soldiers, be guarding their own firesides." As mothers, wives, sisters, and sweethearts of men who fought for the Union and as the beneficiaries of their military triumph, black women identified fully with the contributions of black soldiers to the struggle for freedom. Yet that

---

[72] On the poverty endured by soldiers' families, much of it resulting from the paucity and irregularity of military pay, see *Black Military Experience*, docs. 154–55, 156C, 157A, 158B, 160A, 160E, 170A, 271, 290–94, 314D–E, 315A–B, 338–39, 341. See also *Destruction of Slavery*, doc. 231.

very identification—the celebration of black soldiers as liberators—
widened the social distance between men and women.[73]

The accomplishments of black soldiers reverberated beyond the
family circle. Black soldiers eagerly bore the news of emancipation.
In carrying freedom's sword, they demonstrated that liberty was as
much the product of the black man's valor as it was the white man's
gift. Slaves understood this, and they welcomed black soldiers with
special enthusiasm. Fugitives followed the soldiers' line of march,
bondsmen and women fearful of their owners' wrath sought refuge
with black regiments, and everywhere crowds of black men, women,
and children lined the roads to cheer. Besides bearing the message of
liberty, black soldiers also aided the passage of black people from
slavery to freedom in countless practical ways. They informed freedpeople of their newly won rights, tutored them in the nuances of
federal policy, and elaborated on the opportunities that liberty
offered. Although the message they carried—like the rumored possibility of land—often proved to be an empty promise, it encouraged freedpeople to press their former owners and, indeed, their new
Yankee rulers in ways that expanded freedom.[74]

Black people everywhere rallied to the support of the Sable Arm.
Associations to aid sick and wounded soldiers and to provide for the
widows and orphans of the fallen sprang up throughout the North
and liberated South.[75] Whether formerly enslaved or freeborn, black
civilians welcomed black soldiers into their homes and onto the
podium at public meetings and celebrations. They took pride in the
martial accomplishments of black soldiers and shared the indigni-
ties they suffered at the hands of federal policy makers. The black

[73] For the episode in which Wild invited the slave women to whip their master, see
Destruction of Slavery, doc. 16. For the recruitment order, see *Wartime Genesis: Upper
South,* doc. 205n.

[74] See, for example, *Black Military Experience,* docs. 316–18, 324–25.

[75] Louisville, Kentucky, had at least three such associations: the Louisville Colored
Ladies' Soldiers Aid Society, apparently affiliated with the Methodist church; the Colored Soldiers Aid Society of the Fifth Street Baptist Church; and the Soldiers Aid Society of the Green Street Baptist Church. See *Louisville Daily Union Press,* 7, 9, 17, and
30 Jan. 1865. For a similar association in Washington, D.C., see *Second Annual Report,
of the Freedmen and Soldiers' Relief Association . . .* (Washington, 1864).

and abolitionist press provided an important link between soldiers and the larger community. Reports from black soldiers, mostly chaplains and noncommissioned officers, filled newspaper columns in the free states and the occupied South. They not only provided news of the whereabouts of black units for concerned families and friends, but also told tales of black soldiers in mortal combat with the slaveholding enemy, thereby allowing the larger black community to share in the destruction of slavery. The press publicized and criticized discriminatory Union policies, bringing to the home front the issues of unequal pay, the refusal to commission black officers, and the abuse of black prisoners of war.[76] By counterposing black soldiers' battlefield heroics to the inequities of military life, black leaders put soldiering to work in the struggle for equal rights. After 1863, calls for the end of discrimination rarely failed to mention the importance of black soldiers in defending the Union. Thus for practical as well as emotional reasons, the military experience drew the black community together. Along with emancipation itself, victories on the issues of equal pay and black officers fueled the optimism and sharpened the political consciousness of all black people. Although most black men would not be enfranchised until several years after the war ended, their participation in the politics of reconstruction began with enlistment in the Union army.[77]

The black military experience imparted more than unalloyed optimism. Heroism and self-sacrifice inspired some black soldiers,

---

[76] See, for example, *The Christian Recorder,* New York *Weekly Anglo-African, Douglass' Monthly,* New Orleans *Tribune,* Beaufort *Free South, National Anti-Slavery Standard,* and *The Liberator.* Many letters written by black soldiers for these publications or for hometown newspapers have recently been collected and published. See James Henry Gooding, *On the Altar of Freedom: A Black Soldier's Civil War Letters from the Front,* ed. Virginia Matzke Adams (Amherst, Mass., 1991); Edwin S. Redkey, ed., *A Grand Army of Black Men: Letters from African-American Soldiers in the Union Army, 1861–1865* (Cambridge, U.K., 1992); Noah Andre Trudeau, ed., *Voices of the 55th: Letters from the 55th Massachusetts Volunteers, 1861–1865* (Dayton, Ohio, 1996); George E. Stephens, *A Voice of Thunder: The Civil War Letters of George E. Stephens,* ed. Donald Yacovone (Urbana, Ill., 1997). See also R. J. M. Blackett, ed., *Thomas Morris Chester, Black Civil War Correspondent: His Dispatches from the Virginia Front* (Baton Rouge, La., 1989).

[77] *Black Military Experience,* docs. 362–63, 367; McPherson, *Negro's Civil War,* chaps. 18–19.

but the appalling carnage, the inequities of military life, and the equivocal commitment of federal officials to black advancement left others disillusioned. The experience of black soldiers warned black people that, at best, the Yankees were unreliable allies whose interests only occasionally coincided with those of the black community. The frequent failure of army officers to correct transparent injustices and their willingness to reject the most heart-rending protests on the cold ground of military necessity left black soldiers and civilians alike more distrustful than confident about the white man's army and the white man's government. While this disillusionment estranged some from the political process, it hardened others to the struggle still ahead and deepened their determination to press on. In either case, such attitudes reflected a new sophistication, an understanding that, as in slave times, black people would have to keep their own counsel, that even in the moment of triumph nothing would come easily, and that political victories often cost as much as military ones.

The influence of soldiering on black life did not end when the shooting stopped. If anything, its importance grew. Many black soldiers remained in uniform as part of the Union army of occupation, and they continued to advise freedpeople on the new demands of freedom and the workings of the world beyond the plantation. Their presence, especially when commanded by sympathetic white officers, helped to limit violence against freedpeople and to prevent newly returned Confederate veterans from riding roughshod over defenseless former slaves. Military service also provided a stepping-stone to leadership in the black community. With wartime responsibilities behind them, black soldiers often became deeply involved in the black communities where they were stationed. Some took wives from among the local population and fully entered local community life, thereby fusing the experience of the liberator and the liberated. Drawing on their martial experience and the confidence it engendered, black soldiers framed the aspirations of many of the newly freed and also helped reconstruct the black community's institutions to meet the demands of freedom. They frequently took the lead in establishing schools, building churches, and founding fraternal societies. In the first political conventions held by black people following the war, soldiers played a prominent part. By standing armed and ready to aid black people, and by bringing knowledge and confidence to their communities, black soldiers remained significant figures after emancipation.[78]

In much the same way that the liberating impact of the black military experience radiated from black soldiers and their families into the larger black community, so it spread into white society as well. Abolitionist officers, many of whom had led the fight for black enlistment, provided the most important agents of the dissemination of a new racial liberality. Standing with black soldiers through the war and, in some quarters, suffering from identification with black troops, their commitment to equality inside the army deepened their commitment to equality in American society generally. Many remained in the South as Freedmen's Bureau agents, Republican politicians, and schoolteachers. Others who returned to the North joined with black men, including many who had served under their command, to form a nub of consistent support for racial equality within the Republican party. They attacked second-class citizenship within American society just as they had attacked it in the army. Pointing to the contribution of black soldiers in preserving the Union, they helped roll back the color line

---

[78] On black soldiers in the postwar army of occupation, see *Black Military Experience,* chap. 17; Glatthaar, *Forged in Battle,* chap. 10. On their participation in postemancipation political meetings, which routinely insisted that the wartime service of black soldiers entitled black men to full political rights, see Philip S. Foner and George E. Walker, eds., *Proceedings of the Black State Conventions, 1840–1865,* 2 vols. (Philadelphia, 1979–80), vol. 2, pp. 242–304, and virtually all the meetings included in Philip S. Foner and George E. Walker, eds., *Proceedings of the Black National and State Conventions, 1865–1900,* 1 vol. to date (Philadelphia, 1986–), vol. 1. For black veterans who held political office in the former Confederate states, see Eric Foner, *Freedom's Lawmakers: A Directory of Black Officeholders during Reconstruction* (New York, 1993). On the role of black veterans in postbellum politics more generally, see Eric Foner, *Reconstruction: America's Unfinished Revolution* (New York, 1988), pp. 9–10, 112–19; Glatthaar, *Forged in Battle,* pp. 248–51; Leon F. Litwack, *Been in the Storm So Long: The Aftermath of Slavery* (New York, 1979), chap. 10.

in the Northern states and urged a radical reconstruction of the defeated Confederacy.[79]

White Northerners in growing numbers became convinced that the service of black soldiers on behalf of the Union entitled them to participate formally in governing the reconstructed Confederate states. In the spring of 1864, while nudging conservative Louisiana unionists into a position more consonant with changing congressional sentiment, President Lincoln singled out former soldiers as one category of black men who might be granted the suffrage. In the years that followed, others—whether resisting more extensive changes in the racial status quo or urging still greater ones—drew upon the wartime service of black men to make similar arguments. The black military experience thus expanded and deepened the nation's commitment to equal rights.[80]

Perhaps no one more fully understood the role black soldiers played in inflating the aspirations and enlarging the opportunities of black people than did members of the old master class. Even when they admitted that black soldiers acquitted themselves in an impeccable manner, former slaveholders complained bitterly about the unsettling influence of black troops on the old pattern of subordination. Once freedpeople came in contact with black troops, they deferred less readily and labored less willingly. By their presence as well as their words and actions, black soldiers convinced former slaves and former masters alike that the old world was gone forever.[81]

---

[79] See, for example, the postwar writings of two white officers of black regiments: Norwood P. Hallowell, *The Meaning of Memorial Day* (Boston, 1896), and *The Negro as a Soldier in the War of the Rebellion* (Boston, 1897), both reprinted in *Selected Letters and Papers of N. P. Hallowell* (Peterborough, N.H., 1963); Thomas J. Morgan, *The Negro in America and the Ideal American Republic* (Philadelphia, 1898). See also Glatthaar, *Forged in Battle*, pp. 257–60.

[80] Lincoln, *Collected Works*, vol. 7, p. 243; Mary Frances Berry, *Military Necessity and Civil Rights Policy: Black Citizenship and the Constitution, 1861–1868* (Port Washington, N.Y., 1977), chap. 7; McPherson, *Negro's Civil War*, chap. 19.

[81] *Black Military Experience*, docs. 316–17, 319, 321, 324–25, 28, 330B–C; Litwack, *Been in the Storm So Long*, pp. 267–74. The presence of black soldiers had had similarly disruptive effects in Union-occupied parts of the Confederacy during the war, most notably in southern Louisiana. See, for example, *Destruction of Slavery*, docs. 69–70, 72; *Wartime Genesis: Lower South*, docs. 74, 77, 83.

As black soldiers and civilians gloried in the world turned upside down, former slaveholders detested the revolution and despised black soldiers as symbols of the new state of affairs. They pleaded for the removal of black soldiers from the South, complaining not only of the arrogance or misconduct of the soldiers themselves but also of the social disruption that would certainly follow from the provocative nature of a black military presence. Such appeals, especially when filtered through white unionists, had a powerful influence on federal officials and sped the demobilization of many black units and the relegation of others to distant corners of the South. Where black troops remained in service, white Southerners did not accept their presence easily, and violence between black soldiers and white civilians became commonplace.[82]

While in the ranks of the Union army, black soldiers had protection enough. But once mustered out of service, much of that protection vanished. Black veterans became fair game for white regulators and terrorists, and when they eluded such gangs, their families frequently became the victims of violent abuse. In some areas of the South, attacks on black soldiers and their families approached full-scale pogroms.[83]

Such assaults only confirmed the importance of the black military experience. Brutal attacks on black soldiers reemphasized their centrality in breaking the bonds of servitude and paving the way for freedom. The image of long lines of black soldiers marching through the South with slaveholders fleeing at their approach spurred black people—freeborn and former slave—to seek a fuller freedom and sustained them in the face of continued adversity. Throughout the postwar years, the contributions of black men to Union victory provided a firm basis for claims to equality, and black

[82] For white civilians' objections to and attacks on black soldiers in the postwar army of occupation, see *Black Military Experience,* docs. 316–17, 321–22, 324–25, 327–28, 330A–C.

[83] For examples of attacks on and harassment of black veterans and their families, see *Black Military Experience,* docs. 331, 352–61. For an attempt by one group of veterans to form a militia for self-protection, see *Black Military Experience,* doc. 364.

veterans continued to play a central role in black communities, North and South. The skills and experience black men gained during the war not only propelled many of them into positions of leadership and sustained the prominence of others, but also shaped the expectations and aspirations of all black people. The achievements and pride engendered by military service helped to make a new world of freedom.

Slave into soldier: Private Hubbard Pryor of Georgia before and after his
enlistment in the 44th U.S. Colored Infantry, 1864
(National Archives)

Freemen into soldiers: Sergeant Lewis H. Douglass (opposite) and Private
Charles R. Douglass (above) of the 54th Massachusetts Infantry, sons of
Frederick Douglass
(Moorland-Spingarn Research Center, Howard University)

COLORED SOLDIERS!

EQUAL STATE RIGHTS!

AND MONTHLY PAY WITH WHITE MEN !!

On the 1st day of January, 1863, the President of the United States proclaimed

FREEDOM TO OVER

THREE MILLIONS OF SLAVES!

This decree is to be enforced by all the power of the Nation.   On the 21st of July last he issued the following order :—

PROTECTION OF COLORED TROOPS.

"WAR DEPARTMENT, ADJUTANT GENERAL'S OFFICE, }
WASHINGTON, July 21.   }

" *General Order, No. 233.*

"The following order of the President is published for the information and government of all concerned :—

EXECUTIVE MANSION, WASHINGTON, July 30.

' " It is the duty of every Government to give protection to its citizens, of whatever class, color, or condition, and especially to those who are duly organized as soldiers in the public service.   The law of nations, and the usages and customs of war, as carried on by civilized powers, permit no distinction as to color in the treatment of prisoners of war as public enemies.   To sell or enslave any captured person on account of his color, is a relapse into barbarism, and a crime against the civilization of the age.

' " The Government of the United States will give the same protection to all its soldiers, and if the enemy shall sell or enslave any one because of his color, the offence shall be punished by retaliation upon the enemy's prisoners in our possession.   It is, therefore, ordered, for every soldier of the United States, killed in violation ot the laws of war, a rebel soldier shall be executed; and for every one enslaved by the enemy, or sold into slavery, a rebel soldier shall be placed at hard labor on the public works, and continued at such labor until the other shall be released and receive the treatment due to prisoners of war.

' " ABRAHAM LINCOLN." '

' " By order of the Secretary of War.

' " E. D. TOWNSEND, Assistant Adjutant General." '

That the President is in earnest the rebels soon began to find out, as witness the following order from his Secretary of War :—

" WAR DEPARTMENT, WASHINGTON CITY, August 8, 1863.

" SIR :—Your letter of the 3d inst., calling the attention of this Department to the cases of Orin H. Brown, William H. Johnston, and Wm. Wilson, three colored men captured on the gunboat Isaac Smith, has received consideration.   This Department has directed that three rebel prisoners of South Carolina, if there be any such in our possession, and if not, three others, be confined in close custody and held as hostages for Brown, Johnston, and Wilson, and that the fact be communicated to the rebel authorities at Richmond.

" Very respectfully your obedient servant,

" EDWIN M. STANTON, Secretary of War.

" The Hon. GIDEON WELLES, Secretary of the Navy."

And retaliation will be our practice now—man for man—to the bitter end.

Recruitment poster, 1863
(National Archives)

54

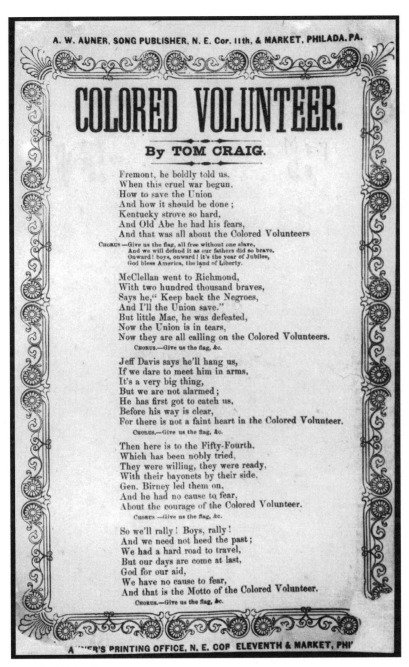

Broadside ballad
(Rare Book Room, Buffalo and Erie County Public Library)

55

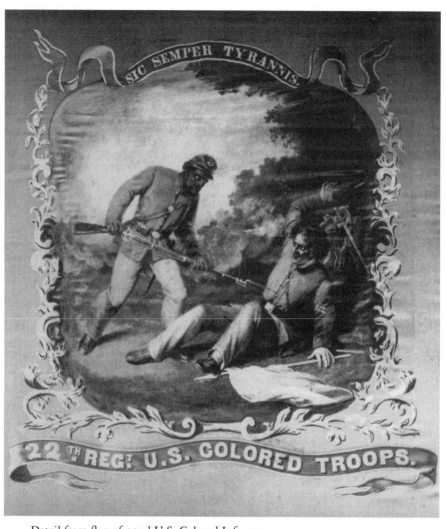

Detail from flag of 22nd U.S. Colored Infantry
(Photography Collections, University of Maryland Baltimore County)

Detail from flag of 3rd U.S. Colored Infantry
(Freedmen and Southern Society Project)

26th U.S. Colored Infantry at Camp William Penn, 1865
(National Archives)

Louisiana black soldiers at Port Hudson, La.
(National Archives)

Color party of 57th U.S. Colored Infantry in Arkansas, ca. 1866
(J. N. Heiskell Historical Collection, University of Arkansas–Little Rock Archives)

Band of 107th U.S. Colored Infantry at Fort Corcoran, Arlington, Va., 1865
(Library of Congress)

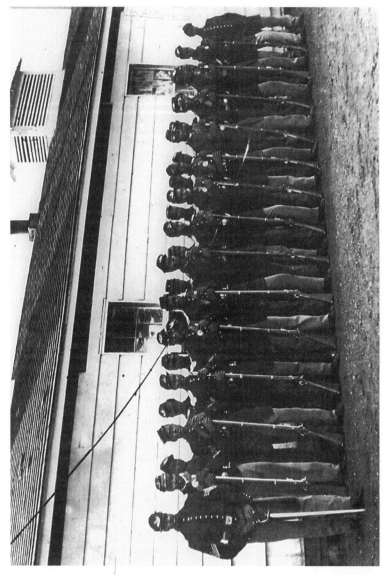

Co. E, 4th U.S.
Colored Infantry at
Fort Lincoln, D.C.
(Library of Congress)

62

Battery A, 2nd
U.S. Colored Artillery
(Lt.) in the Department
of the Cumberland
(Chicago Historical Society)

Black soldiers with their teachers, probably in South Carolina
(Library of Congress)

School for black soldiers and freedpeople at Port Hudson, La. (Chicago Historical Society)

Black sailors sewing and resting on deck of USS *Miami*
(U.S. Naval Historical Center)

Major Martin R. Delany, ca. 1865
(Moorland-Spingarn Research Center, Howard University)

Lieutenant James Monroe Trotter, 1865
(Division of Rare and Manuscript Collections, Cornell University Library)

Unidentified soldier in 55th Massachusetts Infantry
(Alfred S. Hartwell Collection, State Library of Massachusetts)

Unidentified soldier
(Chicago Historical Society)

Unidentified soldier
(Chicago Historical Society)

Charge of black troops on James Island, S.C. (National Archives)

Assault by Louisiana black troops at Port Hudson, La., 27 May 1863
(*Frank Leslie's Illustrated Newspaper*, 27 June 1863)

Assault by the 54th
Massachusetts Infantry
on Fort Wagner, S.C.,
18 July 1863
(Private collection)

Black soldiers lead
Emancipation Day
celebration on Port Royal
Island, S.C., 1 January 1863
(*Frank Leslie's Illustrated
Newspaper*, 24 January 1863)

Black soldiers
liberating slaves
in North Carolina
(*Harper's Weekly*,
23 January 1864)

Former slaves greet the 55th Massachusetts Infantry as it marches into Charleston, S.C., 21 February 1865 (*Harper's Weekly*, 18 March 1865)

Marriage of a
black soldier and
a freedwoman at
Vicksburg, Miss.
(*Harper's Weekly*
30 June 1866)

Black soldiers
mustered out at
Little Rock, Ark.,
1866 (pencil drawing
by Alfred R. Waud)
(Library of Congress)

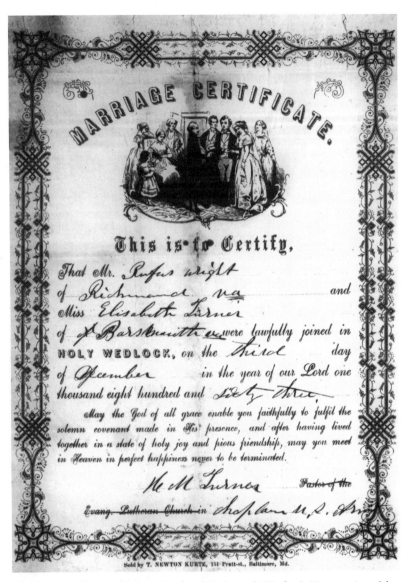

Marriage certificate of Private Rufus Wright and Elisabeth Turner, signed by Henry M. Turner, a minister in the African Methodist Episcopal Church and chaplain of the 1st U.S. Colored Infantry
(National Archives)

An escaped slave in the Union army
(*Harper's Weekly*, 2 July 1864)

2

Freedom's Soldiers: A Documentary History

NORTH AND SOUTH, free and slave, black men clamored to enter the Union army, hoping to strike a blow at slavery and assert their claim for equality. Officials of the Lincoln administration ignored such requests or rejected them outright. The resulting vacuum attracted the attention of Union officers sympathetic to the slaves' cause. One of the officers most determined to make freedom universal was General David Hunter, the federal military commander in the Union-occupied sea islands of South Carolina. In May 1862, Hunter issued his own proclamation of emancipation, freeing slaves in South Carolina, Georgia, and Florida. Although President Lincoln promptly voided that edict, Hunter went on to enlist ex-slaves as soldiers without War Department authorization. When a congressional resolution sponsored by border-state representatives demanded an explanation, Hunter retorted that he had no fugitive slaves under arms, only men "whose late masters are 'Fugitive Rebels.'" Hunter's letter quickly became a featured story in the antislavery press, which employed his withering sarcasm to good effect.

Port Royal   S⁰ C⁰   June 23rd 1862

Sir: I have the honor to acknowledge the receipt of a
communication from the Adjutant General of the Army, dated
June 13th 1862, requesting me to furnish you with information
necessary to answer certain resolutions introduced in the
House f Representatives, June 9th 1862, on motion of the Hon.
Mr. Wickliffe of Kentucky,—their substance being to inquire;

1st   Whether I had organized or was organizing a regiment
of "Fugitive Slaves" in this Department.

2nd   Whether any authority had been given to me from the
War Department for such organization;—and

3rd   Whether I had been furnished by order of the War
Department with clothing, uniforms, arms, equipments and
so forth for such a force?

Only having received the letter covering these inquiries at a
late hour on Saturday night, I urge forward my answer in
time for the Steamer sailing today (Monday),—this haste
preventing me from entering as minutely as I could wish
upon many points of detail such as the paramount
importance of the subject calls for.   But in view of the near
termination of the present session of Congress, and the widespread interest which must have been awakened by Mr
Wickliffe's Resolutions, I prefer sending even this imperfect
answer to waiting the period necessary for the collection of
fuller and more comprehensive data.

To the First Question therefore I reply that no regiment of
"Fugitive Slaves" has been, or is being organized in this
Department.   There is, however, a fine regiment of persons
whose late masters are "Fugitive Rebels,"—men who
everywhere fly before the appearance of the National Flag,
leaving their servants behind them to shift as best they can
for themselves.—   So far, indeed, are the loyal persons
composing this regiment from seeking to avoid the presence
of their late owners, that they are now, one and all, working

with remarkable industry to place themselves in a position to go in full and effective pursuit of their fugacious and traitorous proprietors.

To the Second Question, I have the honor to answer that the instructions given to Brig. Gen. T. W. Sherman by the Hon. Simon Cameron, late Secretary of War, and turned over to me by succession for my guidance,—do distinctly authorize me to employ all loyal persons offering their services in defence of the Union and for the suppression of this Rebellion in any manner I might see fit, or that the circumstances might call for.   There is no restriction as to the character or color of the persons to be employed, or the nature of the employment, whether civil or military, in which their services should be used.   I conclude, therefore that I have been authorized to enlist "Fugitive Slaves" as soldiers, could any such be found in this Department.—   No such characters, however, have yet appeared within view of our most advanced pickets,—the loyal slaves everywhere remaining on their plantations to welcome us, aid us, and supply us with food, labor and information.—   It is the masters who have in every instance been the "Fugitives", running away from loyal slaves as well as loyal soldiers, and whom we have only partially been able to see,—chiefly their heads over ramparts, or, rifle in hand, dodging behind trees,—in the extreme distance.—   In the absence of any "Fugitive Master Law", the deserted Slaves would be wholly without remedy, had not the crime of Treason given them the right to pursue, capture and bring back those persons of whose protection they have been thus suddenly bereft.

To the Third Interrogatory, it is my painful duty to reply that I never have received any Specific authority for issues of clothing, uniforms, arms, equipments and so forth to the troops in question,—my general instructions from Mr Cameron to employ them in any manner I might find necessary, and the military exigencies of the Department and the country, being my only, but in my judgment, sufficient justification.   Neither have I had any Specific authority for supplying these persons with shovels, spades and pick axes when employing them as laborers, nor with boats and oars when using them as lightermen,—but these are not points included in Mr. Wickliffe's Resolution.—   To me it seemed that liberty to employ men in any particular capacity implied with it liberty, also, to supply them with the necessary tools; and acting upon this faith, I have clothed, equipped and armed the only loyal regiment yet raised in South Carolina.

I must say, in vindication of my own conduct, that had it not been for the many other diversified and imperative claims on my time and attention, a much more satisfactory result might have been hoped for; and that in place of only one, as at present, at least five or six well-drilled, brave and thoroughly acclimated regiments should by this time have been added to the loyal forces of the Union.

The experiment of arming the Blacks, so far as I have made it, has been a complete and even marvellous success.   They are sober, docile, attentive and enthusiastic, displaying great natural capacities for acquiring the duties of the soldier.   They are eager beyond all things to take the field and be led into action; and it is the unanimous opinion of the officers who have had charge of them, that in the peculiarities of this climate and Country they will prove invaluable auxiliaries,—fully equal to the similar regiments so long and successfully used by the British Authorities in the West India Islands.

In conclusion I would say it is my hope,—there appearing no possibility of other reinforcements owing to the exigencies of the Campaign in the Peninsula,—to have organized by the end of next Fall, and to be able to present to the Government,

from forty eight to fifty thousand of these hardy and devoted
soldiers.— Trusting that this letter may form part of your
answer to Mr Wickliffe's Resolutions, I have the honor to be,
most respectfully, Your Very Obed^t Servt.

HLc   [*David Hunter*]

∽

By the summer of 1862, tens of thousands of black men and
women were employed by the Union army as guides, spies,
teamsters, laborers, cooks, laundresses, and hospital atten-
dants. They performed all manner of work, from preparing
camps to constructing fortifications. Northerners could not
help but recognize the importance of former slaves to the
war effort. Their successful employment as laborers pushed
to the fore the possibility of using them as soldiers: If black
men could wield a shovel they could also shoulder a musket. Many Northerners who cared little about emancipation
and racial equality thus came to favor the enlistment of
black soldiers on utterly pragmatic grounds. In a letter to
General-in-Chief Henry W. Halleck, Governor Samuel J.
Kirkwood of Iowa suggested that a black man could stop a
bullet as well as a white man.

[*Des Moines*] Iowa   August 5 1862
General   You will bear me witness I have not trouble on the
"*negro*" subject but there is as it seems to me so much good
sense in the following extract from a letter to me from one of
the best colonels this state has in the service that I have

yielded to the temptation to send it to you— It is as follows. "I hope under the confiscation and emancipation bill just passed by Congress[1] to supply my regiment with a sufficient number of 'contrabands'[2] to do all the 'extra duty' labor of my camp. I have now *sixty men on extra duty* as teamsters &c. whose places could just as well be filled with *niggers*— We do not need a single negro in the army to fight but we could use to good advantage about one hundred & fifty with a regiment as teamsters & for making roads, chopping wood, policing camp &c. *There are enough soldiers on extra duty in the army to take Richmond or any other rebel city if they were in the ranks instead of doing negro work."*

I have but one remark to add and that in regard to the negroes fighting— it is this—When this war is over & we have summed up the entire loss of life it has imposed on the country I shall not have any regrets if it is found that a part of the dead are *niggers* and that *all* are not white men—

. . . .

ALS   Samuel J Kirkwood

The Northern armies that left winter quarters for the spring campaigns of 1863 marched under a new banner, for emancipation had become central to federal military policy. Not only were former slaves working as laborers in the Union cause, but black men were also entering armed service under the provisions of Lincoln's Emancipation Proclamation. Recognizing the importance of slavery to the Confed-

---

[1] The Second Confiscation Act and the Militia Act. (See page 6.)
[2] That is, former slaves.

eracy and the value of ex-slaves to the Union, most Northerners had come to regard the mobilization of black laborers
and soldiers as militarily necessary. From the War Department in Washington, General Henry W. Halleck privately
advised General Ulysses S. Grant about the changing pur-
poses of the war and the military benefits of emancipation.
As a general in the field, Halleck had steadfastly disavowed
interference with slavery, and he felt little enthusiasm for
the new policy. Nevertheless, he too acknowledged that
measures once thought radical had become common sense.

Washington [*D.C.*],   March 31ˢᵗ /63
(Unofficial)
Genl,   It is the policy of the government to withdraw from
the enemy as much productive labor as possible.   So long as
the rebels retain and employ their slaves in producing grains,
&c, they can employ all the whites in the field.   Every slave
withdrawn from the enemy, is equivalent to a white man put
hors de combat.[3]

Again, it is the policy of the government to use the negroes
of the South so far as practicable as a military force for the
defence of forts, depôts, &c.   If the experience of Genl Banks
near New Orleans should be satisfactory, a much larger force
will be organized during the coming summer; & if they can be
used to hold points on the Mississippi during the sickly season,
it will afford much relief to our armies.   They certainly can be
used with advantage as laborers, teamsters, cooks, &c.

And it is the opinion of many who have examined the
question without passion or prejudice, that they can also be
used as a military force.   It certainly is good policy to use
them to the very best advantage we can.   Like almost

---

[3] Out of combat; disabled.

anything else, they may be made instruments of good or
evil. In the hands of the enemy they are used with much
effect against us. In our hands we must try to use them with
the best possible effect against the rebels.

It has been reported to the Secretary of War that many of
the officers of your command not only discourage the
negroes from coming under our protection, but, by ill
treatment, force them to return to their masters. This is not
only bad policy in itself, but it is directly opposed to the
policy adopted by the government. Whatever may be the
individual opinion of an officer in regard to the wisdom of
measures adopted and announced by the government, it is
the duty of every one to cheerfully and honestly endeavour to
carry out the measures so adopted. Their good or bad
policy is a matter of opinion before they are tried; their real
character can only be determined by a fair trial. When
adopted by the government it is the duty of every officer to
give them such a trial, and to do everything in his power to
carry the orders of his government into execution.

It is expected that you will use your official and personal
influence to remove prejudices on this subject, and to fully
and thoroughly carry out the policy now adopted and
ordered by the government. That policy is, to withdraw
from the use of the enemy all the slaves you can, and to
employ those so withdrawn, to the best possible advantage
against the enemy.

The character of the war has very much changed within the
last year. There is now no possible hope of a reconciliation
with the rebels. The union party in the South is virtually
destroyed. There can be no peace but that which is enforced
by the sword. We must conquer the rebels, or be conquered
by them. The north must either destroy the slave-oligarchy,
or become slaves themselves;—the manufacturers—mere
hewers of wood and drawers of water to southern aristocrats.

This is the phase which the rebellion has now assumed. We must take things as they are. The government, looking at the subject in all its aspects, has adopted a policy, and we must cheerfully and faithfully carry out that policy.

I write you this unofficial letter, simply as a personal friend, and as a matter of friendly advice. From my position here, where I can survey the entire field, perhaps I may be better able to understand the tone of public opinion, and the intentions of the Government, than you can from merely consulting the officers of your own army. Very respectfully Your obt servt

HLdS   H. W. Halleck

∾

Although the Emancipation Proclamation provided that black men would "be received into the armed service of the United States,"[4] it did not specify the terms and conditions under which they would serve. The governor of Massachusetts assured George T. Downing, a black businessman and prominent abolitionist, that black soldiers would stand on an equal footing with white soldiers.

Boston [*Mass.*], March 23. 1863.
Dear Sir: In reply to your inquiries made as to the position of colored men who may be enlisted and mustered into the volunteer service of the United States, I would say, that their position, in respect to pay, equipments, bounty, or aid and

[4] *Statutes at Large*, vol. 12, pp. 1268–69.

protection, when so mustered, will be precisely the same, in every particular, as that of any and all other volunteers.

I desire further to state to you, that when I was in Washington, on one occasion, in an interview with Mr Stanton, the Secretary of War, he stated in the most emphatic manner, that he would never consent that free colored men should be accepted into the service to serve as soldiers in the South until he should be assured that the Government of the United States was prepared to guarantee and defend, to the last dollar and the last man, to these men, all the rights, privileges and immunities that are given, by the laws of civilized warfare, to other soldiers.   Their present acceptance and muster-in, as soldiers, pledges the honor of the Nation in the same degree and to the same rights with all other troops.   They will be soldiers of the Union—nothing less and nothing different.   I believe they will earn for themselves an honorable fame, vindicating their race and redeeming their future from disaspersions of the past.   I am yours truly,
HLcSr   John A. Andrew.

∽

Promises of equal treatment were broken time and again, exposing the limits of the Union's commitment to equality. The exclusion of black men from the commissioned ranks— lieutenant and higher—was a case in point. At the end of 1862, Union troops in southern Louisiana included regi- ments of "Native Guards" composed in part of freemen of African descent and most of whose officers were also free men of color. A few companies had served in the militia under the Confederacy, but when federal troops occupied

New Orleans they declared their allegiance to the Union. In August 1862, General Benjamin F. Butler incorporated them into his command and began recruiting to augment their ranks. Butler's successor, General Nathaniel P. Banks, accepted the regiments but not their officers, whom he considered unfit to hold commissioned rank. Early in 1863, Banks began forcing them to resign, and within months all but a handful had complied. Demobilized but not demoralized, they reiterated their desire to serve the Union. Invoking their long tradition of military service, including the valorous conduct of their forefathers during the War of 1812, they urged Banks to reconsider his position.

New Orleans [*La.*]   April 7ᵗʰ 1863

Sir   we the undersigned in part resigned officers of the Third (3ʳᵈ) regᵗ La vol native guards and others desiring to assist in putting down this wicked rebelion. And in restoring peace to our once peaceful country. And wishing to share with you the dangers of the battle field and serve our country under you as our forefathers did under [*Andrew*] Jackson in eighteen hundred and fourteen and fifteen—On part of the ex officers we hereby volunteer our services to recruit A regiment of infantry for the United Satates army—   The commanding Genˡ may think that we will have the same difficulties to surmount that we had before resigning.   But sir give us A commander who will appreciate us as men and soldiers, And we will be willing to surmount all outer difficulties   We hope allso if we are permitted to go into the service again we will be allowed to share the dangers of the battle field and not be Kept for men who will not fight   If the world doubts our fighting give us A chance and we will show then what we can do—   We transmit this for your

perusal and await your just conclusion. And hope that you
will grant our request   We remain respectfuly your
obedient servants

	Adolph. J. Gla	James. E. Moore
	Samuel. Lauence	William. Hardin
	Joseph G Parker	William. Moore
	Joseph. W. Howard	Charles. A. Allen
ALS	Charles. W. Gibbons	Danl W. Smith Jr

∾

To refute persistent charges that they would not fight, black
soldiers were eager to prove themselves under fire. In three
bloody battles during mid-1863—Port Hudson (Louisiana)
in May, Milliken's Bend (Louisiana) in June, and Fort Wagner (South Carolina) in July—they silenced the doubters.
Their conduct not only sealed the federal government's
commitment to enlisting as many black soldiers as possible,
but also guaranteed them a role in the front line. Furthermore, participation in combat established the soldiers'
claim upon the nation. In a letter to the chief recruiter of
black troops in southern Louisiana, a Union officer reported
the bravery of the black soldiers at Port Hudson, many of
whom had until recently been slaves.

Baton Rouge [La.]   May 29th /63.
General.   feeling deeply interested in the cause which you
have espoused, I take the liberty to transmit the following,
concerning the colored Troops engaged in the recent battles at
Port Hudson.

I arrived here the evening of the 26ᵗʰ Inst, was mustered and reported to Maj. Tucker for duty—

During the night I heard heavy connonadeing at Port Hudson.   Early next morning I obtained permission and went to the front. But was so much detained, I did not reach our lines until the fighting for the day had nearly ceased—   There being no renewal of the engagement the following day—I engaged in removing and administering to the wounded, gathering meantime as much information as possible concerning the battle and the conduct of our Troops.   My anxiety was to learn all I could concerning the Bravery of the Colored Reg. engaged, for their good conduct and bravery would add to your undertakings and make more popular the movement.   Not that I am afraid to meet unpopular doctrins, for I am not. But that we may show our full strength. the cause should be one of general sanction.

I have ever believed, from my idea of those traits of character which I deemed necessary to make a good soldier, together with their history, that in them we should find those characteristics necessary, for an effictive army.   And I rejoice to learn, in the late engagements the fact is established beyond a doubt.

The following is (in substance) a statement personally made to me, by 1ˢᵗ Lt. Co. F. 1ˢᵗ R[*egiment*]. La. Native Guard who was wounded during the engagement.

"We went into action about 6. A.M. and was under fire most of the time until sunset.

The very first thing after forming line of battle we were ordered to charge—   My Co. was apparrently brave. Yet they are mostly contrabands, and I must say I entertained some fears as to their pluck.   But I have now none—   The moment the order was given, they entered upon its execution.   Valiantly did the heroic decendants of Africa move forward cool as if Marshaled for dress parade, under a most murderous fire from the enemies guns, until we reached the main ditch which surrounds the Fort. finding it impassible we retreated under orders to the woods and deployed as skirmishers— In the charge we lost our Capt. and Colored sergeant, the latter fell wraped in the flag he had so gallantly borne— Alone we held our position until 12. o'clock when we were relieved—

At two o'clock P.M. we were again ordered to the front where we made two separate charges each in the face of a heavy fire from the enemies Battery of seven guns—whose destructive fire would have confuse and almost disorganized the bravest troops. But these men did not swerve, or show cowardice. I have been in several engagements, and I never before beheld such coolness and darring—

Their gallantry entitles them to a special praise. And I already observe, the sneers of others are being tempered into eulogy—"

It is pleasant to learn these things, and it must be indeed gratifying to the General to know that his army will be composed of men of almost unequaled coolness & bravery—

The men of our Reg. are very ready in learning the drills, and the officers have every confidence in their becoming excellent soldiers.

Assureing you that I will always, both as an officer of the U.S. Army and as a man, endeavor to faithfully & fully discharge the duties of my office, I am happy to Subscribe Myself, Very Respectfully, Your Most Obt. Servt,

ALS   Elias D. Strunke

∾

At Milliken's Bend, another post on the Mississippi River, untested black soldiers joined a white regiment in hand-to-hand combat with Confederate troops who had vowed to show the black men and their officers no mercy. The commander of the District of Northeastern Louisiana described the battle to his superiors.

Young's Point, La.,   June 12", 1863.
Colonel: I have the honor to report, that in accordance with instructions recieved from me, Colonel Leib, Commanding 9" La. A[*frican*]. D[*escent*]. made a reconnaisance in the direction of Richmond, on June the 6th starting from Milliken's Bend at 2 A.M.   He was preceeded by two Companies of the 10" Illinois Cavalry, Commanded by Captain Anderson, whom he overtook three miles from the Bend.   It was agreed between them that the Captain should take the left side of Walnut Bayou, and pursue it as far as Mrs. Ame's Plantation, while Colonel Leib proceeded along the Main Richmond road to the Railroad Depot, three (3) miles from Richmond, where he encountered the enemies Pickets and advance, which he drove in with but little opposition, but anticipating the enemy in strong force, retired slowly toward the Bend.   When about half way back, a squad of our Cavalry came dashing up in his rear, hotly pursued by the enemy.—   Colonel Leib immediately formed his regiment across an open field, and with one volley, dispersed the approaching enemy.   Expecting the enemy would contest the passage of the Bridge over Walnut Bayou, Colonel Leib fell back over the bridge, and from thence to Milliken's Bend, from whence he sent a Messenger informing me of the success of the expedition, and reported the enemy to be advancing.   I immediately started the 23" Iowa

Vol. Inft. to their assistance, and Admiral Porter ordered the Gun-Boat "Choctow" to that Point.

At three (3) o'clock the following morning the enemy made their appearance, in strong force, on the Main Richmond road, driving the Pickets before them.   The enemy advanced upon the left of our line—throwing out no skirmishers—Marching in close column, by division, with a strong Cavalry force on his right flank.   Our forces—consisting of the 23d Iowa Vol. Inft. and the African Brigade, in all, 1061 men—opened upon the enemy when within musket-shot range, which made them waver and recoil; a number running in confusion to the rear, the balance, pushing on with intrepidity, soon reached the Levee, when they were ordered to "charge," with cries of "No Quarters!"   The African Regiments being inexperienced in use of arms—some of them having been drilled but a few days, and the guns being very inferior—the enemy succeeded in getting upon our works before more than one or two volleys were fired at them.   Here ensued a most terrible hand to hand conflict, of several minutes duration, our men using the bayonet freely and clubbing their guns with fierce obstinacy, contesting every inch of ground, until the enemy succeeded in flanking them and poured a murderous enfilading fire along our lines—directing their fire chiefly to the officers, who fell in numbers.   Not 'till they were overpowered, and forced by superior numbers, did our men fall back behind the bank of the river, at the same time pouring volley after volley into the ranks of the advancing enemy

The Gun-Boat now got into position and fired a broad-side into the enemy, who immediately disappeared behind the Levee, but all the time keeping up a fire upon our men

The enemy at this time appeared to be extending his line to the extreme right, but was held in check by two Companies of the 11" La. Inft. A[frican]. D[escent]., which had been posted behind cotton bales and part of the old Levee.   In this position the fight continued until near noon, when the enemy suddenly withdrew.   Our men seeing this movement, advanced upon the retreating column, firing volley after volley at them, while they remained within gun-shot.   The Gun-Boat "Lexington" then paid her compliments to the "flying foe," in several well directed shots, scattering them in all directions.   I here desire to express my thanks to the officers and men of the Gun-Boats "Choctaw" and "Lexington" for their efficient services in the time of need.   Their names will long be remembered by the officers and men of the "African Brigade," for their valuable assistance on that dark and bloody field.

The officers and men deserve the highest praise for their gallant conduct, and especially Colonel Glasgow of the 23^{d} Iowa, and his brave men, and also Colonel Leib, of the 9" La., A[*frican*]. D[*escent*]. , who by his gallantry and daring, inspired his men to deeds of valor, until he fell, seriously, though not dangerously wounded.   I regret to state that Col. Chamberlain, of the 11" La. A[*frican*]. D[*escent*]. , conducted himself in a very unsoldierlike manner.

The enemy consisted of one (1) Brigade, numbering about 2,500, in command of General McCullough, and two hundred Cavalry.   The enemies loss is estimated at about 150 killed, and 300 wounded.   It is impossible to get anything near the loss of the enemy, as they carried killed and wounded off in ambulances.   Among their killed is Colonel Allen, 16" Texas.

Enclosed please find tabular statements of killed, wounded and missing—in all 652.   Nearly all the missing Blacks will probably return, as they were badly scattered

The enemy, under General Hawes, advanced upon Youngs Point whilst the battle was going on at Milliken's Bend, but several well-directed shots from the Gun-Boat's compelled them to retire.

Submitting the foregoing, I remain Yours Respectfully,

HLS   Elias S. Dennis

Paying rueful tribute to the black soldiers who fought at Milliken's Bend, a Confederate officer reported that they had resisted "with considerable obstinacy, while the white or true Yankee portion ran like whipped curs."⁵

☙

Among those who questioned the ability of black soldiers to fight were high-ranking Northern officers, including General Quincy A. Gillmore, who commanded the Department of the South. But the performance of the 54th Massachusetts Infantry in the ill-fated—and, some thought, ill-advised—assault on Fort Wagner, South Carolina, in July 1863 changed many minds. Several months after the battle, Nathaniel Paige, a correspondent for the *New-York Tribune* who had witnessed the engagement, testified before a War Department commission about its effect on prevailing prejudices.

[*New Orleans, La.   February? 1864*]
. . . .

Gen. Gilmore had little confidence in negro troops when he assumed command of the Department; Col. Turner was Chief of Staff; Maj. Smith was assistant Adjutant General; his generals were Terry, Seymour, Strong, Vogdes, Stevenson, Gordon and Wilde; the colored troops were in Strong's brigade; the bombardment of Fort Wagner commenced at 11 A.M. from the iron-clad fleet and all the shore batteries; the

⁵ *Official Records*, ser. 1, vol. 24, pt. 2, p. 467.

action continued until about an hour before sunset, with occasional replies from Wagner and Sumter; Gen. Seymour had command; Gen. Gilmore with his staff, the leading colonels, and the correspondents of the press, were on the observatory, 2 1/2 miles from Sumter and 1 3/4 from Wagner. An hour before sunset, Gen. Gilmore (who had been most of the time on the observatory) came down and asked Gen. Seymour (who was lying on the ground) if he thought the fort could be taken by assault. Gen. Seymour replied: "I can run right over it. I can camp my whole command there in one night." Said Gen. Gilmore: "Very well. If you think you can take it you have permission to make the assault. How do you intend to organize your command?" Gen. Seymour answered: "Well, I guess we will let Strong lead and put those d----d niggers from Massachusetts in the advance; we may as well get rid of them, one time as another. But," said he, "I would give more for my old company of regulars than for the whole d----d crowd of volunteers." Gen. Gilmore laughed, but ordered the movement to take place. Gen. Seymour's command were soon formed in line of battle on the beach in front of the town; 1 3/4 miles from Wagner. The division was organized by placing Gen. Strong in advance, Col. Putnam second and Gen. Stevenson in reserve. The whole column moved together up to a house about a mile from Fort Wagner, in open daylight and in full view of the enemy from all the forts; there all halted but the brigade of Gen. Strong; he marched up at double quick towards the fort, under a most terrific fire from Forts Gregg and Sumter and all the James Island batteries, losing on the way 150 killed and wounded. The first brigade assaulted at dusk, the 54th Massachusetts in the front. Col. Shaw was shot just as he mounted the parapet of the fort. Notwithstanding the loss of their Colonel, the regiment pushed forward, and more than

one-half succeeded in reaching the inside of the fort. Three
standard bearers were shot, but the flag was held by the
regiment until their retreat. The regiment went into action
commanded by their Colonel and a full staff of officers; it
came out led by Second Lieut Higginson—a nephew of Col.
H—he being the highest officer left to command, all ranking
being either killed or wounded. Gen. Strong's brigade was
led out by Maj. Plimpton of the 3d New Hampshire. Gen.
Strong received a mortal wound almost at the commencement
of the action; Col. Shaw was killed, and all the other colonels
severely wounded. The 1st brigade having been repulsed
with such severe loss, the second brigade was then ordered to
move. Col. Putnam led his brigade gallantly; carried the
flag of the 7th New Hampshire into the fort, which he held
for half an hour without being reinforced. The enemy
succeeded in bringing to bear against him ten or twelve brass
howitzers, loaded with grape and canister, when the
slaughter became so terrible that he was forced to retire, after
having lost nearly all his officers. About fifty of the 54th
Massachusetts were taken prisoners; none have been
exchanged; I believe all reports as to the harsh treatment of
our colored prisoners are untrue; I have reason to think that
they are treated as prisoners of war. Gen. Gilmore and staff
ridiculed negro troops; the evident purpose in putting the
negroes in advance was to dispose of the idea that the
negroes could fight; Major Smith advised Gen. Gilmore to put
the negroes at the head of the assaulting party and get rid of
them. On the previous week Gen. Terry had made favorable
mention of the 54th Massachusetts for gallantry on James
Island. Many of Gen. Terry's officers spoke of them
unfavorably before and favorably since the action referred
to. The regiment is now at Morris Island; numbers four
hundred men; is in Col. Littlefield's brigade and is
commanded by Major Hallowell. Gen. Seymour was not in

the advance at Fort Wagner, but early in the action received a very slight wound in his heel, not drawing blood, immediately after which he retired to the south end of Morris Island and remained there all night; next morning he congratulated the remaining officers upon their escape, and charged the failure of the assault upon the d----d negroes from Massachusetts. He is now an ardent admirer of negro troops. These facts are personally known to me, and I am willing to swear to their truth.

. . . .

HD

∽

The coincidence of large-scale enlistment of black men in the Union army and Northern victories at Vicksburg, Mississippi, and Gettysburg, Pennsylvania, caused the Confederates to fear for the worst. With Union forces now in control of the entire Mississippi River, slaveholders transferred (or "refugeed," as the process was called) tens of thousands of slaves to the interior rather than lose them to the Yankees. The large-scale removals undermined slave discipline and placed enormous burdens upon the resources of interior regions. Such desperate times called for desperate measures, a Mississippi planter advised Confederate President Jefferson Davis, including, if need be, the induction of slave men into the Confederate army.

Louisville Miss   July 20th /63
Dear Sir   Visburg is gone and as a consequence Mississippi is gone and in the opinion of allmost every one here the

Confederacy is gone.   I can myself see but one chance, but one course to pursue to pursue to save it, and I fear it is now too late for even that to check the tide that is overwhelming us.   It is simply by your own authority, and without waiting for congress to give you authority, to call out every able bodied *Negro* man from the age of sixteen to fifty years old.   They will go readily and cheerfully.   The owners would gladly give them up and afford every facility in getting them off.   On every road leading from the western Country there is a constant stream of negroes running into Ala & Georgia & the Carolinas.   They will destroy all the food in those states like an army of locusts.   This if nothing else would starve us into subjection in a few months   It is precisly what our enemy want.   Take our nego men away and thereby relieve us of a dangerous element.   Force the young white men, who are running off with them, into the army and we, the old men will take care of the negro women and children and make corn.   Act promptly   the negro men will all go to the enemy if not taken to our own army   I believe fully half of them had rather go into our ranks than the Yankees   They want to be in the frollick & they will be one way or the other.   Away with all squeamesness about employing negroes in civilized warfare.   Our enemies are doing it as rappidly as they can and we are left no other alternative.—   If you knew with what pleasure I would send off every negro man I have tomorrow morning you would not dismiss this hastily.   I am only one of the masses and what I say I believe nearly every slave holder in the South would say and do.   With the highest considerations of respect I am verry truly youre friend.
ALS   O G Eiland

Far from sharing Eiland's confidence that slaves would will-ingly fight for the rebel cause, most Confederates feared that, given the opportunity, their bondsmen would take up arms for the Union. Forcible evacuation of able-bodied slaves from endangered areas seemed the only way to prevent them from joining the Northern army. "Every sound male black left for the enemy," warned one Confederate general in September 1863, "becomes a soldier whom we have afterwards to fight."[6]

∽

The participation of black soldiers in combat engendered fear about the treatment they would receive if they were captured by the Confederates. The fear was well-founded, for Confederate authorities from the first refused to recognize armed black men as soldiers and, instead, declared them slaves in insurrection. At first, local commanders decided the fate of captured black soldiers, often executing them on the spot. In December 1862, however, Confederate President Jefferson Davis ordered that thereafter they be delivered to civil authorities to be dealt with according to state laws,[7] under which they faced punishments ranging from enslavement to execution. Shortly after the battle of Fort Wagner, the mother of a soldier in the 54th Massachusetts Infantry urged President Lincoln to guarantee the proper treatment of captured black soldiers. In measured but heartfelt words she defined the president's responsibilities to the soldiers and their families and demanded that he fulfill them.

[6] Lt. Gen. E. Kirby Smith to Maj. Genl. Price, 4 Sept. 1863, *Destruction of Slavery*, p. 772.
[7] *Official Records*, ser. 2, vol. 5, p. 797.

Buffalo [*N.Y.*]   July 31 1863

Excellent Sir   My good friend says I must write to you and
she will send it   My son went in the 54th regiment.   I am a
colored woman and my son was strong and able as any to
fight for his country and the colored people have as much to
fight for as any.   My father was a Slave and escaped from
Louisiana before I was born morn forty years agone   I have
but poor edication but I never went to schol, but I know just as
well as any what is right between man and man.   Now I
know it is right that a colored man should go and fight for his
country, and so ought to a white man.   I know that a colored
man ought to run no greater risques than a white, his pay is no
greater his obligation to fight is the same.   So why should not
our enemies be compelled to treat him the same, Made to do it.

My son fought at Fort Wagoner but thank God he was not
taken prisoner, as many were   I thought of this thing before
I let my boy go but then they said M^r. Lincoln will never let
them sell our colored soldiers for slaves,   if they do he will
get them back quck   he will rettallyate and stop it.   Now
Mr Lincoln dont you think you oght to stop this thing and
make them do the same by the colored men   they have
lived in idleness all their lives on stolen labor and made
savages of the colored people, but they now are so furious
because they are proving themselves to be men, such as have
come away and got some edication.   It must not be so.   You
must put the rebels to work in State prisons to making shoes
and things, if they sell our colored soldiers, till they let them
all go.   And give their wounded the same treatment.   it
would seem cruel, but their no other way, and a just man
must do hard things sometimes, that shew him to be a great
man.   They tell me some do you will take back the
[*Emancipation*] Proclamation,   don't do it.   When you are
dead and in Heaven, in a thousand years that action of yours
will make the Angels sing your praises I know it.   Ought one

Buffalo July 31 1863

Excellent Sir

My good friend says I must write to you and she will send it   My son went in the 54th regiment, I am a colored woman and my son was strong and able as any to fight for his country and the colored people have as as much to fight for as any, My father was a slave and escaped from Louisiana before I was born morn forty years agonce I know but poor education but I never went to school, but I know just as well as any what is right between man and man . Now I know it is right that a Colored man should go and fight for his Country, and so ought to a white man , I know that a Colored Man ought to run no greater risques than a White, his pay is no greater his obligation to fight is the same. So why should not our enemies be compelled to treat him the same, Made to do it ,

My son fought at Fort Wagoner but thank god he was not taken prisoner, as many were

First page of letter from Hannah Johnson to President Abraham Lincoln (see p. 106).

n another, law for or not,   who made the law,
poor slave did not.   so it is wicked, and a horrible
there is no sense in it,   because a man has lived by
ll his life and his father before him, should he
n because the stolen things found on him are
taken.   Robbing the colored people of their labor is but a
small part of the robbery   their souls are almost taken, they
are made bruits of often.   You know all about this
    Will you see that the colored men fighting now, are fairly
treated.   You ought to do this, and do it at once, Not let the
thing run along   meet it quickly and manfully, and stop
this, mean cowardly cruelty.   We poor oppressed ones,
appeal to you, and ask fair play.   Yours for Christs sake

                                        Hannah Johnson.
[*In another handwriting*]   Hon. Mr. Lincoln   The above
speaks for itself   Carrie Coburn
ALS

Unbeknown to Hannah Johnson, Lincoln had only the previous day promised to retaliate against Confederate prisoners if captured black soldiers were denied the rights of prisoners of war.[8]

ᖰᖱ

When black soldiers went to war, they did so for reasons that
differed from those of many Northerners. In a document
found in a street in New Orleans, an anonymous "Colored

[8] *Official Records*, ser. 2, vol. 6, p. 163.

man" insisted that saving the Union was a hollow objective
unless accompanied by the destruction of slavery. He further
maintained that discrimination within the Union army and
the continuing legality of slavery in southern Louisiana—a
region exempted from the Emancipation Proclamation—
made it difficult for people of African descent to identify
their interests fully with those of the Union.

[*New Orleans, La. September? 1863*]
. . . .

it is retten that a man can not Serve two master But it
Seems that the Collored population has got two a rebel
master and a union master   the both want our
Servises   one wants us to make Cotton and Sugar And the
Sell it and keep the money   the union masters wants us to
fight the battles under white officers and the injoy both
money and the union   black Soldiers And white officers
will not play togeathe much longer   the Constitution is if
any man rebells against those united States his property Shall
be confescated and Slaves declared and henceforth Set free
forever   when theire is a insurection or rebllion against
these united States the Constitution gives the president of the
united States full power to arm as many soldiers of African
decent as he deems nescesisary to Surpress the Rebellion and
officers Should be black or white According to their
abillitys   the Collored man Should guard Stations Garison
forts and mand vessels according to his Compasitys
    A well regulated militia being necessary to the cecurity of a
free State the right of the people to keep and Bear arms Shall
not be infringed
    we are to Support the Constitution but no religious test
Shall ever be required as a qualification to Any office or

public trust under the united States   the excitement of the
wars is mostly keep up from the Churches   the Say god is
fighting the battle but it is the people   But the will find that
god fought our battle once   the way to have peace is to
distroy the enemy   As long as theire is a Slave their will be
rebles Against the Government of the united States   So we
must look out our white officers may be union men but Slave
holders at heart   the Are allways on hand when theire is
money but Look out for them in the battle feild   liberty is
what we want and nothing Shorter

   our Southern friend tells that the are fighting for negros
and will have them   our union friends Says the are not
fighting to free the negroes   we are fighting for the union
and free navigation of the Mississippi river   very well let
the white fight for what the want and we negroes fight for
what we want   there are three things to fight for and two
races of people divided into three Classes   one wants negro
Slaves the other the union the other Liberty   So liberty
must take the day nothing Shorter   we are the Blackest and
the bravest race   the president Says there is a wide
Difference Between the black Race and the white race   But
we Say that white corn and yellow will mix by the taussels
but the black and white Race must mix by the roots as the are
so well mixed and has no tausels—freedom and liberty is the
word with the Collered people

· · · ·

Sure the Southern men Says the are not fighting for money
the are fighting for negros   the northern men Say the did
not com South to free the negroes but to Save the
union   very well for that much   what is the colored men
fighting for   if the makes us free we are happy to hear it
And when we are free men and a people we will fight for our
rights and liberty   we care nothing about the union   we
heave been in it Slaves over two hundred And fifty

years   we have made the contry and So far Saved the union
and if we heave to fight for our rights let us fight under
Colored officers for we are the men that will kill the Enemies
of the Government

. . . .

now is the united States government and constitution free
or a local Goverment   if it is free let us colored population
muster in to ams and garison forts guard Station and mand
vessels and then we will know wheather we are free people
or not   then we will know wheather you want to make
brest works of us or not or make us fools ornot   I heard one
of most Ables and distingush lawiers Say that the Colored
population was all free and Had as much liberty in the union
as he had   in four or five days after I went to him to get him
to atend Some buiness for me   he Said to me Are you free
or Slave   Sir Said i am free By your own speeches   was
you born free   no Sir Said i   we have been made fools of
from the time Butlers fleet landed hear but I have remained
At my old Stand and will untill i See what i am dowing   I
know very well that the white union men cannot put down
the rebeles for them that was not rebles Soon will be   i am
Sory that I am not able to write good   may the union
forever Stand with peace and liberty to All good people
HD   A Colored man

ও

As the "Colored man" knew, black soldiers could not always
rely upon their professed friends in the North. Disregarding
promises of equal treatment, the government often
employed black soldiers as little more than uniformed
drudges. Many white soldiers and officers simply assumed

that black soldiers would and should do the dirty work.
Colonel James C. Beecher, a member of a prominent antislavery family and the commander of a regiment of former
slaves from North Carolina, protested to his brigade commander the harmful effects of such assignments.

Folly Island [S.C.]   Sept. 13th 1863.

General   It is reported to me on good authority that men of
my command ordered to Morris Island on fatigue duty, are
put to work laying out and policing camps of white soldiers
on that Island.   I am informed that to day a detachment of 60
men properly officered, having been ordered to report to a
Major Butts of some New York Regiment were set to work
levelling ground for the Regimental Camp, digging wells &c
pitching tents and the like.

Since the commencement of the war I have never before
known such duty imposed upon any Regiment; it being
(unless I am greatly in error) the custom of New York and
other Regiments to pitch their own tents and lay out their
own camps a privilege, by the way, which my men have had
little time to enjoy by reason of constant detail on fatigue.

As you are aware—the fatigue duty of my regiment has
been incessant and trying—so that my sick list has increased
from 4 or 5 to nearly 200 in a little over one month; and I
respectfully protest against the imposition of labors which by
no principle of custom or right devolve upon my
command.   I respectfully protest against this particular
imposition because of its injurious influence upon the men in
another respect.

They have been slaves and are just learning to be men   It
IS a draw-back that they are regarded as, and called "d----d
Niggers" by so-called "gentleman" in uniform of U.S.
Officers, but when they are set to menial work doing for

white regiments what those Regiments are entitled to do for themselves, it simply throws them back where they were before and reduces them to the position of slaves again.

I therefore request that you will entertain this my protest; and, if you find no objection to the matter or manner of the same, will forward it through the proper Channel to the General Commanding the Department— If these men do their duty in the trenches, and in the field, I do not believe that he will make them hewers of wood and drawers of water for those who do no more. I am General Very Respectfully Yours
HLcSr   James C. Beecher

Favorable endorsements by Beecher's superiors—one of whom, however, found the complaint "wanting in proper respect"—resulted in orders prohibiting the use of black soldiers "to prepare camps and perform menial duties for white troops" in the Department of the South.[9] Similar protests by black soldiers and their officers in other commands eventually led the adjutant general of the army, in June 1864, to order that black troops "only be required to take their fair share of fatigue duty, with the white troops."[10]

‿

Of all the inequities black soldiers endured, the most galling resulted from the Militia Act of July 1862. Primarily intended to govern the mobilization of fugitive slaves as military laborers, the law authorized the president to employ

9 *Black Military Experience*, p. 494.
10 *Black Military Experience*, pp. 500–501.

"persons of African descent" at $10 per month ($3 of which could be deducted for clothing).[11] It was not immediately apparent that these provisions would apply to black soldiers. Until the summer of 1863, all Union privates—black and white—collected $13 per month (plus an allotment of clothing or its equivalent cash value of $3.50); noncommissioned and commissioned officers drew higher amounts. But in June of that year, the army began paying all black soldiers—whether freemen or ex-slaves, and regardless of rank—in conformity with the Militia Act. That decision ignited a firestorm of protest that raged for a full year. Writing directly to the president, a freeborn corporal in the 54th Massachusetts Infantry eloquently stated his comrades' case for equal pay; he emphasized in particular the injustice of applying to Northern freemen a law meant for former slaves.

Morris Island [S.C.].   Sept 28th 1863.
Your Excelency will pardon the presumtion of an humble individual like myself, in addressing you. but the earnest Solicitation of my Comrades in Arms, besides the genuine interest felt by myself in the matter is my excuse, for placing before the Executive head of the Nation our Common Grievance: On the 6th of the last Month, the Paymaster of the department, informed us, that if we would decide to recieve the sum of $10 (ten dollars) per month, he would come and pay us that sum, but, that, on the sitting of Congress, the Regt would, in his opinion, be *allowed* the other 3 (three.)   He did not give us any guarantee that this would be, as he hoped, certainly *he* had no authority for making any such guarantee, and we can not supose him acting in any way interested.   Now the main question is. Are we *Soldiers*, or are we LABOURERS.   We are fully armed, and equipped, have done

11 *Statutes at Large*, vol. 12, pp. 597–600.

all the various Duties, pertaining to a Soldiers life, have
conducted ourselves, to the complete satisfaction of General
Officers, who, were if any, prejudiced *against* us, but who now
accord us all the encouragement, and honour due us: have
shared the perils, and Labour, of Reducing the first stronghold,
that flaunted a Traitor Flag: and more, Mr President.   Today,
the Anglo Saxon Mother, Wife, or Sister, are not alone, in tears
for departed Sons, Husbands, and Brothers.   The patient
Trusting Decendants of Africs Clime, have dyed the ground
with blood, in defense of the Union, and Democracy.   Men too
your Excellency, who know in a measure, the cruelties of the
Iron heel of oppression, which in years gone by, the very
Power, their blood is now being spilled to maintain, ever
ground them to the dust.   But When the war trumpet
sounded o'er the land, when men knew not the Friend from
the Traitor, the Black man laid his life at the Altar of the
Nation,—and he was refused.   When the arms of the Union,
were beaten, in the first year of the War, And the Executive
called more food. for its ravaging maw, again the black man
begged, the privelege of Aiding his Country in her need, to be
again refused,   And now, he is in the War: and how has he
conducted himself?   Let their dusky forms, rise up, out the
mires of James Island, and give the answer.   Let the rich
mould around Wagners parapets be upturned, and there will
be found an Eloquent answer.   Obedient and patient, and
Solid as a wall are they.   all we lack, is a paler hue, and a
better acquaintance with the Alphabet.   Now Your Excellency,
We have done a Soldiers Duty.   Why cant we have a Soldiers
pay?   You caution the Rebel Chieftain, that the United States,
knows, no distinction, in her Soldiers: She insists on having
all her Soldiers, of whatever, creed or Color, to be treated,
according to the usages of War.   Now if the United States
exacts uniformity of treatment of her Soldiers, from the
Insurgents, would it not be well, and consistent, to set the

example herself, by paying all her *Soldiers* alike?   We of this Regt. were not enlisted under any "contraband" act.   But we do not wish to be understood, as rating our Service, of more Value to the Government, than the service of the exslave,   Their Service *is* undoubtedly worth much to the Nation, but Congress made express, provision touching their case, as slaves freed by military necessity, and assuming the Government, to be their temporary Gaurdian:—   Not so with us—Freemen by birth, and consequently, having the advantage of *thinking,* and acting for ourselves, so far as the Laws would allow us.   We do not consider ourselves fit subjects for the Contraband act.   We appeal to You, Sir: as the Executive of the Nation, to have us Justly Dealt with.   The Regt, do pray, that they be assured their service will be fairly appreciated, by paying them as american SOLDIERS, not as menial hierlings.   Black men You may well know, are poor,   three dollars per month, for a year, will suply their needy Wives, and little ones, with fuel.   If you, as chief Magistrate of the Nation, will assure us, of our whole pay. We are content, our Patriotism, our enthusiasm will have a new impetus, to exert our energy more and more to aid Our Country.   Not that our hearts ever flagged, in Devotion, spite the evident apathy displayed in our behalf, but We feel as though, our Country spurned us, now we are sworn to serve her.

   Please give this a moments attention

ALS   James Henry Gooding

∽

Corporal Gooding hinted at the hardship endured by black soldiers' families in the free states, but the families of their

comrades from the border states, where slavery was still
legal, suffered even greater trials. Many wives, children, and
parents of border-state soldiers remained in the custody of
slaveholders embittered by the men's enlistment. Martha
Glover of Missouri described to her husband the burdens
she had borne since he joined the army.

Mexico Mo   Dec 30th 1863

My Dear Husband   I have received your last kind letter a
few days ago and was much pleased to hear from you once
more.   It seems like a long time since you left me.   I have
had nothing but trouble since you left.   You recollect what I
told you how they would do after you was gone.   they abuse
me because you went & say they will not take care of our
children & do nothing but quarrel with me all the time and
beat me scandalously the day before yesterday—   Oh I never
thought you would give me so much trouble as I have got to
bear now.   You ought not to left me in the fix I am in & all
these little helpless children to take care of.   I was invited to
a party to night but I could not go   I am in too much
trouble to want to go to parties.   the children talk about you
all the time.   I wish you could get a furlough & come to see
us once more.   We want to see you worse than we ever did
before.   Remember all I told you about how they would do
me after you left—for they do worse than they ever did & I
do not know what will become of me & my poor little
children.   Oh I wish you had staid with me & not gone till I
could go with you for I do nothing but grieve all the time
about you.   write & tell me when you are coming.

Tell Isaac that his mother come & got his clothes   she was
so sorry he went.   You need not tell me to beg any more
married men to go.   I see too much trouble to try to get any

more into trouble too— Write to me & do not forget me & my children— farewell my dear husband from your wife

ALS   Martha

∽

Although the tribulations of black soldiers' families remained, for the most part, private, the abuse of captured soldiers claimed the attention of the Northern public. In a notorious episode, on April 12, 1864, Confederate troops commanded by General Nathan Bedford Forrest captured the federal garrison at Fort Pillow, Tennessee, and then slaughtered scores of Union soldiers who had already surrendered, most of whom were black. The atrocity sparked a congressional investigation and demands that President Lincoln make good his threat of retaliation. Failure to do so, a black New Yorker warned the secretary of war, would alienate black Americans from the Union cause.

New York [N.Y.] April 18th 1864

Sir: Some Sixty or Seventy thousand of my down trodden and despised brethren now wear the uniform of the United States and are bearing the gun and sword in protecting the life of this once great nation   with this in view I am emboldened to address a few words to you in their behalf if not in behalf of the government itself.   Jeff Davis issued a threat that black men fighting for the U.S. should not be treated as prisoners of war and the President issued a proclamation threatening retaliation.[12]   Since then black soldiers have been murdered

12 See pages 105, 108.

again and again yet where is there an instance of retaliation. To be sure there has been a sort of secrecy about many of these slaughters of colored troops that prevented an official declaration to be made but there is now an open and bold murder, an act following the proclaimed threat made in cold blood gives the government an opportunity to show the world whether the rebels or the U.S. have the strongest power. If the murder of the colored troops at Fort Pillow is not followed by prompt action on the part of our government. it may as well disband *all its colored troops* for no soldiers whom the goverment will not protect can be depended upon Now Sir if you will permit a colored man to give not exactly advice to your excellency but the expression of his fellow colored men so as to give them heart and courage to believe in their goverment you can do so by a prompt retaliation. Let the same no. of rebel soldiers, privates and officers be selected from those now in confinement as prisoners of war captured at the west and let them be surrounded by two or three regiments of colored troops who may be allowed to open fire upon them in squads of 50 or 100, with howitzers loaded with grape. The whole civilized world will approve of this necessary military execution and the rebels will learn that the U.S. Govt. is not to be trifled with and the black men will feel not a spirit of revenge for have they not often taken the rebels prisoners even their old masters without indulging in a fiendish spirit of revenge or exultation. Do this sir *promptly and without notice to the rebels at Richmond* when the *execution has* been made then an official declaration or explanation may be made. If the threat is made first or notice given to the rebels they will set apart the same no. for execution. Even that mild copperhead[13]

---

[13] "Copperhead" was a derogatory term for a Northerner who supported or sympathized with the Confederacy.

Reverdy Johnston avowed in a speech in the Senate that this
govt. could only be satisfied with man for man as an act of
retaliation.   This request or suggestion is not made in a spirit
of vindicativeness but simply in the interest of my poor
suffering confiding fellow negros who are even now
assembling at Annapolis [*Md.*] and other points to reinforce
the army of the Union   Act first in this matter   afterward
explain or threaten   the act tells   the threat or demand is
regarded as idle.   I am Sir with great respect Your humble
Servant.

ALS   Theodore Hodgkins

Discussions between President Lincoln and his cabinet
about responding to the Fort Pillow massacre resulted in a
decision to retaliate only against actual offenders from Forrest's command, should any be captured, but to warn the
Confederate government that a number of captured Southern officers would be held as hostages against such actions
in the future. The policy, however, was not put into effect.[14]

∽

The appointment of black men to military positions that
entailed authority over white men was unacceptable to federal officials, white soldiers, and the Northern public. The
cashiering of the Louisiana black officers in 1863[15] reflected
that hostility, and until early 1865 the War Department
steadfastly refused to commission black men as line officers,

[14] James M. McPherson, *Battle Cry of Freedom: The Civil War Era* (New York, 1988), p.
794.
[15] See pages 92–94.

no matter what their qualifications. They nevertheless continued to press for commissions, if not as captains and lieu-
tenants then as chaplains and surgeons. And because the
latter positions did not involve battlefield command, the
War Department received such applications with somewhat
more favor. The former slave of a prominent secessionist
sought the endorsement of Secretary of State William H.
Seward for his appointment to a chaplaincy.

Camp Casey   Washington City [*D.C.*] May 18th 1864
dear sir   please parden me for troubling you with business
that is not Immediately connected with your office, yet it
being justice to myself & of interest to my comrads in the
military service of the government, I hope your honor will at
once pardon me for the liberty I take in writing you such a
letter.   You will judge from past correspondence whilst in
Canada that I was anxious to serve my country to the best of
my humble ability.   I have recruited colored men for every
colored regiment raised in the north forsaken my church in
ohio & canvassed the intire north & west urging my people to
inlist & have succeded in every instant at various times were
told that I would have the chaplaincy of some one of the
colored Regiment.   I nearly recruited half the men in the 28th
U.S. Colored Infrantry Regiment raised in Indiana   Gov
O. P. Morton of Ind promised to give me the office *but* could
not as it was transfered from the volunteer serv to that of the
regular Army.   my officers have me acting as a chaplain but
no man seeke my commission.   I pray you will see me
justified after having done as much as I have in raising such
troops.   I refer you to Gov Andrew of Mass Todd of ohio
Morton of Ind Seymore of New York & Spridge of Rhode
I—   I also joined the regt as a private to be with my boys &
should I fail to get my commission I shall willingly serve my

time out, but I know you can get me my commission if any
other gentleman in the world can & at the same time feel
quite certain that should you vail to give my humble plea due
consideration no other will.   I pray you will aid me sprining
from so humble an origin as myself namely that of being the
body servant of Robert Toombs.   please let your humble
servant hear from you as soon as possible.   May heaven
Bless you & family in all your future pursuits   I am dear sir
your very humble servant

ALS   Garland. H. White

> Seward endorsed White's application, and the following
> October, pursuant to his election as chaplain by the regi-
> ment's commissioned officers, White was appointed to the
> position.[16]

∽

> No matter what their rank, black soldiers—like white
> ones—treasured their memories of home and family. Steal-
> ing a quiet moment before going on picket duty, Private
> Ruphus Wright described a recent battle to his wife.

                              wilson Creek Va   May 25th 1864
dear wife   I take the pleasant opportunity of writeing to you
a fiew lines to inform you of the Late Battle we have
had   we was a fight on Tuesday five hours   we whipp the
rebls out   we Killed $200 & captured many Prisener   out

---

[16] *Black Military Experience*, p. 349.

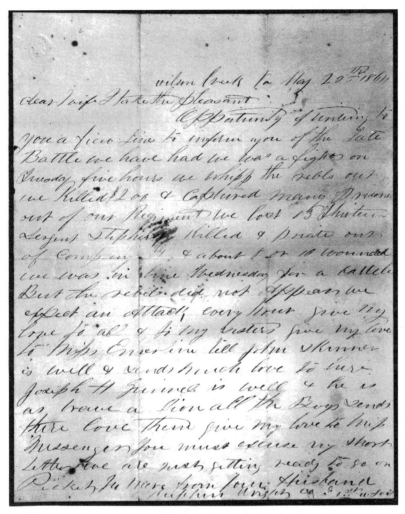

Letter from Private Ruphus Wright to his wife Elisabeth (see pp. 122–24).

of our Regiment we lost 13 Thirteen Sergent Stephensen killed
& priate out of Company H & about 8 or 10 wounded   we
was in line Wednesday for a battele But the rebels did not
Appear   we expect an Attack every hour   give my love to
all & to my sisters give my love   to Miss Emerline tell John

123

Skinner is well & sends much love to her.   Joseph H Grinnel is well & he is as brave a lion   all the Boys sends there love them   give my love to Miss Missenger   You must excuse my short Letter   we are most getting ready to go on Picket   No more from your Husband

ALS   Ruphus Wright

∾

While black soldiers fought, bled, and died for the Union, they continued to receive less pay than their white comrades. Men recruited under explicit promises of equal compensation took particular offense, and, as a result, regiments from the South Carolina sea islands and members of the regiments organized in Massachusetts figured prominently in protests that swept through the ranks. Soldiers in the Massachusetts regiments refused as a matter of principle to accept any pay at all until they were accorded equal pay. They also rejected an offer by the state legislature to make up the difference. Their forthright stand came at considerable cost, often including the impoverishment of their families. More than a year after they opened their protest, believing that the government had still not acted to correct the injustice, members of the 55th Massachusetts Infantry petitioned President Lincoln for immediate discharge and settlement of accounts.

Folly island   South Carolina   July 16th 18.64

Sir   We The Members of Co D of the 55th Massechusetts vols Call the attention of your Excellency to our case

1st   First We wase enlisted under the act of Congress of July 18.61 Placing the officers non Commissioned officers & Privates of the volunteer forces in all Respects as to Pay on the footing of Similar Corps of the Regular Army   2nd   We Have Been in the Field now thirteen months & a Great many yet longer   We Have Recieved no Pay & Have Been offered only seven Dollars Pr month Which the Paymaster Has said was all He Had ever Been authorized to Pay Colored Troops   this was not acording to our enlistment   Consequently We Refused the Money   the Commonwealth of Massechusetts then Passed an act to make up all Deficienceys which the general Government Refused To Pay But this We Could not Recieve as The Troops in the general service are not Paid Partly By Government & Partly By State   3rd   that to us money is no object   we came to fight For Liberty justice & Equality.   These are gifts we Prise more Highly than Gold   For these We Left our Homes our Famileys Friends & Relatives most Dear to take as it ware our Lives in our Hands To Do Battle for God & Liberty

4th   after the elaps of over thirteen months spent cheerfully & willingly Doing our Duty most faithfuly in the Trenches Fatiegue Duty in camp and conspicious valor & endurence in Battle as our Past History will Show

P 5th   therefore we Deem these sufficient Reasons for Demanding our Pay from the Date of our inlistment & our imediate Discharge Having Been enlisted under False Prentence as the Past History of the Company will Prove

6th   Be it further Resolved that if imediate steps are not taken to Relieve us we will Resort to more stringent mesures

We have the Honor to Remin your Obedint Servants   The members of Co D

HLS   [*74 signatures*]

In fact, responding at last to demands for equal pay, Congress had on June 15 increased the compensation of black privates to $13 per month (the same as white privates) and provided that higher-ranking black soldiers receive the same pay as their white counterparts. For men who had been free before the war, the change was retroactive to the time of their enlistment; for those who had been slaves, to January 1, 1864.[17]

∽

Some 36,000 black soldiers died in the service of their country during the Civil War. Disease claimed eleven men for each one who succumbed to battlefield wounds. Contributing to the high incidence of disease was the presumption by federal authorities that people of African descent were physiologically adapted to tropical climates and peculiarly suited to duty in unhealthy settings. The assignment of many black soldiers to endless rounds of arduous fatigue duty further endangered their health. In an unsigned letter to an unnamed official, a soldier from New York described the toll that hard labor and short rations were taking on his regiment.

New Orleans   Camp Parpit   Louisiana   [*August*] 1864
My Dear Friend and x Pre   I thake up my Pen to Address
you A fiew simpels And facts   We so called the 20th u.s.
Colored troops we was got up in the state of New York so
said By A grant of the President.   we Dont think he know
wether we are white or Black   we have not Bin Organized

[17] *Statutes at Large*, vol. 13, pp. 129–30.

yet And A grate meney Brought Away without Being
Musterd in, and we are treated in a Different maner to what
others Rigiments is Both Northern men or southern Raised
Rigiment   Instead of the musket It is the spad and the
Whelbarrow and the Axe   cuting in one of the most horable
swamps in Louisiana stinking and misery   Men are Call to
go on thes fatiuges wen sum of them are scarc Able to get
Along the Day Before on the sick List And Prehaps weeks to
And By this treatment meney are thowen Back in sickness
wich thay very seldom get over.   we had when we Left New
York over A thousand strong   now we scarce rise Nine
hundred the total is said to Be   we lost 1.60 men who have
Left thire homes friends and Relation And Come Down hear
to Lose thire Lives in For the Country thy Dwll in or stayd
in   the Colored man is like A lost sheep   Meney of them
old and young was Brave And Active. But has Bin hurrided
By and ignominious Death into Eternity.   But I hope God
will Presearve the Rest Now in existance to Get Justice and
Rights   we have to Do our Duty or Die and no help for
us   It is true the Country is in A hard strugle   But we All
must Remember Mercy and Justice Grate and small.   it is
Devine.   we All Listed for so much Bounty Clothing and
Ration And 13 Dollars A month.   And the most has fallen
short in all thes Things   we havent Recived A cent of Pay
Since we Bin in the field.   Instead of them Coming to us Like
men with our 13 Dollars thay come with only seven Dollars A
month wich only A fiew tuck it   we stand in Need of
Money very much indeed And think it is no more than Just
an Right we should have it   And Another thing we are Cut
short of our Ration in A most Shocking maner.   I wont Relate
All now But we Are Nerly Deprived of All Comforts of
Life   Hardly have Anough Bread to Keep us From
starving   six or 8 ounces of it to Do A Soldier 24 hours on
Gaurd or eney other Labor and About the Same in Meat and

Coffee   sum times No meat for 2 Days   soup meat Licqour
with very Little seazing the Boys calls hot water or meat tea
for Diner   It is A hard thing to be Keept in such a state of
misery Continuly   It is spoken Dont musel the ox that
treads out the corn.   Remember we are men standing in
Readiness to face thous vile traitors an Rebeles who are trying
to Bring your Peaceable homes to Destruction.   And how
can we stand them in A weak and starving Condition
HL

∽

Black soldiers who fell in battle earned special honor, especially in the eyes of their comrades. A soldier from Maryland
consoled the mother of a friend who had died in combat.

Near Petersburge [*Va.*]   August 19th 1864
Dear Madam   I receave A letter from You A few day Ago
inquir in regard to the Fait of Your Son   I am sarry to have
to inform You that thear is no dobt of his Death   he Died A
Brave Death in Trying to Save the Colors of Rige[*ment*] in that
Dreadful Battil   Billys Death was unevesally [*mourned*] by
all but by non greatter then by my self   ever sins we have
bin in the Army we have bin amoung the moust intimoat
Friend   wen every our Rige[*ment*] wen into Camp he sertan
to be at my Tent and meney happy moment we seen to gether
Talking about Home and the Probability of our Living to get
Home to See each other Family and Friend   But Providence
has will other wise and You must Bow to His will   You and
His Wife Sister and all Have my deepust Simppathy and trust
will be well all in this Trying moment

You Inquired about Mr Young   He wen to the Hospetol and I can not give You eney other information in regard to Him

Billys thing that You requested to inquired about I can git no informa of as in the bustil of the Battil every thing was Lost

Give my Respects to Samual Jackson and Family not forgeting Your self and Family   I remain Your Friend

ALS   G. H. Freeman

༄

Undaunted by the perils of battle against a slaveholding foe, black soldiers also risked their lives in direct assaults on slavery. The commander of a black brigade in eastern Virginia reported the outcome when a detachment of his men escorted a group of military laborers on a dangerous expedition to liberate family and friends.

Newport-News, Va.   Sept. 1st, 1864.

Sir,   I have the honor to report that some Government employees (colored) came up here from Fort Monroe and Hampton Hospitals, having been allowed a short leave of absence for the purpose of getting their families if possible.   I told them I had no boats, but would help them with men.   They reappeared the next day with sailboats.   I sent with them a Captain and 15 men (dismounted Cavalry).   The families were in and about Smithfield.   I gave them strict instructions to abstain from plundering—to injure no one if possible—to get the women and children merely, and come away as promptly as possible.   They were

to land in the night.   They followed these directions closely:
but became delayed by the numbers of women and children
anxious to follow, whom they packed in extra boats, picked
up there, and towed along.   They also had to contend
against a head tide, and wind calm.   So that their progress
down Smithfield Creek in the early morn was exceedingly
slow.   The inhabitants evidently gathered in from some
concerted plan of alarm or signals.   For, 3 miles below, the
party were intercepted by a force of irregular appearance,
numbering about 100—having horses and dogs with them;—
armed variously with shot guns, rifles, &c, and posted behind
old breastworks with some hurried additions.   They
attacked the leading boats, killed a man and woman, and
wounded another woman therein.   The contrabands then
rowed over to the opposite bank and scattered over the
marshes.   How many more have been slaughtered we know
not.   Two (2) men have since escaped to us singly.—   When
the rear boats, containing the soldiers, came up, the Captain
landed, with the design of attacking the rebels.   But then the
firing revealed their full numbers.   He found they
outnumbered him, more than 6 to 1, and that the REVOLVERS of
our Cavalry, in open boats or on the open beach, would stand
no chance against their rifles behind breastworks.   He
embarked again, and they made their way past the danger, by
wading his men behind the boats, having the baggage and
bedding piled up like a barricade.   They then had a race
with 3 boats, which put out from side creeks to cut them
off.   But for the coolness and ingenuity of Capt. Whiteman,
none would have escaped.   None of the soldiers are known
to have been severely wounded; but 3 are missing in the
marshes and woods.   We have since learned that there are
signal Stations in that neighborhood—which ought to be
brooken up.   I would also earnestly recommend the burning

of a dozen or 20 houses in accordance with *your* General
Order No. 23.[18]   Very respectfully Your obt. Servant
HLS   Edwd A. Wild

∾

Drawing strength from both the Union's commitment to
emancipation and its march toward victory, a black soldier
from Missouri assured first his daughters and then the
woman who owned one of them that the federal army
would do the Lord's work, and that he would be there when
it did. The moment of liberation was at hand.

[*Benton Barracks Hospital, St. Louis, Mo., September 3, 1864*]
My Children   I take my pen in hand to rite you A few lines
to let you know that I have not forgot you and that I want to
see you as bad as ever   now my Dear Children I want you to
be contented with whatever may be your lots   be assured
that I will have you if it cost me my life   on the 28th of the
mounth. 8 hundred White and 8 hundred blacke solders
expects to start up the rivore to Glasgow and above there thats
to be jeneraled by a jeneral that will give me both of
you   when they Come I expect to be with, them and expect
to get you both in return.   Dont be uneasy my children   I
expect to have you.   If Diggs dont give you up this
Government will and I feel confident that I will get

[18] Issued on August 20, 1864, by the commander of the District of Eastern Virginia,
the order announced that Confederate guerrillas thereafter captured in an adjoining
section of North Carolina were to be treated as spies rather than prisoners of war, and
that citizens who aided the guerrillas would be imprisoned and their houses burned.
(*Destruction of Slavery*, p. 99n.)

you   Your Miss Kaitty said that I tried to steal you   But I'll
let her know that god never intended for man to steal his own
flesh and blood.   If I had no cofidence in God I could have
confidence in her   But as it is If I ever had any Confidence in
her I have none now and never expect to have   And I want
her to remember if she meets me with ten thousand soldiers
she [will?] meet her enemy   I once [*thought*] that I had some
respect for them but now my respects is worn out and have no
sympathy for Slaveholders.   And as for her cristianantty I
expect the Devil has Such in hell   You tell her from me that
She is the frist Christian that I ever hard say that aman could
Steal his own child especially out of human bondage
     You can tell her that She can hold to you as long as she
can   I never would expect to ask her again to let you come
to me because I know that the devil has got her hot set
againsts that that is write   now my Dear children I am a
going to close my letter to you   Give my love to all
enquiring friends   tell them all that we are well and want to
see them very much and Corra and Mary receive the greater
part of it you sefves   and dont think hard of us not sending
you any thing   I you father have a plenty for you when I
see you   Spott & Noah sends their love to both of
you   Oh! My Dear children how I do want to see you
HL   [*Spotswood Rice*]

[*Benton Barracks Hospital, St. Louis, Mo., September 3, 1864*]
     I received a leteter from Cariline telling me that you say I
tried to steal to plunder my child away from you   now I
want you to understand that mary is my Child and she is a
God given rite of my own and you may hold on to hear as
long as you can but I want you to remembor this one thing
that the longor you keep my Child from me the longor you
will have to burn in hell and the qwicer youll get their   for

we are now makeing up a bout one thoughsand blacke troops
to Come up tharough and wont to come through Glasgow
and when we come wo be to Copperhood rabbels and to the
Slaveholding rebbels for we dont expect to leave them there
root neor branch   but we thinke how ever that we that have
Children in the hands of you devels we will trie your
[vertues?] the day that we enter Glasgow   I want you to
understand kittey diggs that where ever you and I meets we
are enmays to each orthere   I offered once to pay you forty
dollers for my own Child but I am glad now that you did not
accept it   Just hold on now as long as you can and the
worse it will be for you   you never in you life befor I came
down hear did you give Children any thing not eny thing
whatever not even a dollers worth of expencs   now you call
my children your pro[*per*]ty   not so with me   my
Children is my own and I expect to get them and when I get
ready to come after mary I will have bout a powrer and
autherity to bring hear away and to exacute vengencens on
them that holds my Child   you will then know how to talke
to me   I will assure that and you will know how to talk rite
too   I want you now to just hold on to hear if you want
to   iff your conchosence tells thats the road go that road
and what it will brig you to kittey diggs   I have no fears
about geting mary out of your hands   this whole
Government gives chear to me and you cannot help your self
ALS   Spotswood Rice

∽

Nothing eradicated the prejudices of white soldiers as effectively as black soldiers performing well under fire. And
nothing inspired black soldiers to fight as desperately as the

fear that capture meant certain death. Colonel James S. Brisbin, who supervised the recruitment of black soldiers in Kentucky, described to his superiors how the "jeers and taunts" of white soldiers were silenced by their black comrades' bravery.

Lexington Ky Oct 20 / 64

General   I have the honor to forward herewith a report of the operations of a detachment of the 5th U.S. Colored Cavalry during the late operations in Western Virginia against the Salt Works.

After the main body of the forces had moved, Gen'l Burbridge Comdg District was informed I had some mounted recruits belonging to the 5th. U.S. Colored Cavalry, then organizing at Camp Nelson and he at once directed me to send them forward.

They were mounted on horses that had been only partly recruited[19] and that had been drawn with the intention of using them only for the purpose of drilling.   Six hundred of the best horses were picked out, mounted and Col Jas. F. Wade 6th. U.S.C. Cav'y was ordered to take command of the Detachment.

The Detachment came up with the main body at Prestonburg Ky and was assigned to the Brigade Commanded by Colonel R. W. Ratliff 12th O[hio]. V. Cav.

On the march the Colored Soldiers as well as their white Officers were made the subject of much ridicule and many insulting remarks by the White Troops and in some instances petty outrages such as the pulling off the Caps of Colored Soldiers, stealing their horses etc was practiced by the White Soldiers.   These insults as well as the jeers and taunts that

---

[19] That is, disabled or diseased horses that had been only partly rehabilitated.

they would not fight were borne by the Colored Soldiers
patiently or punished with dignity by their Officers but in no
instance did I hear Colored soldiers make any reply to
insulting language used toward [*them*] by the White Troops.

On the 2ᵈ of October the forces reached the vicinity of the
Salt Works and finding the enemy in force preparations were
made for battle.   Col Ratliffs Brigade was assigned to the left
of the line and the Brigade dismounted was disposed as
follows.   5ᵗʰ U.S.C. Cav. on the left. 12ᵗʰ O[*hio*]. V. C[*avalry*]. in
the centre and 11ᵗʰ Mich. Cav. on the right.   The point to be
attacked was the side of a high mountain, the Rebels being
posted about half way up behind rifle pits made of logs and
stones to the height of three feet.   All being in readiness the
Brigade moved to the attack.   The Rebels opened upon them
a terrific fire but the line pressed steadily forward up the
steep side of the mountain until they found themselves
within fifty yards of the Enemy.   Here Col. Wade ordered his
force to charge and the Negroes rushed upon the works with
a yell and after a desperate struggle carried the entire line
killing and wounding a large number of the enemy and
capturing some prisoners   There were four hundred black
soldiers engaged in the battle. one hundred having been left
behind sick and with broken down horses on the march, and
one hundred having been left in the Valley to hold
horses.   Out of the four hundred engaged, one hundred and
fourteen men and four officers fell killed or wounded.   Of
this fight I can only say that men could not have behaved
more bravely.   I have seen white troops fight in twenty-
seven battles and I never saw any fight better.   At dusk the
Colored Troops were withdrawn from the enemies works,
which they had held for over two hours, with scarcely a
round of ammunition in their Cartridge Boxes.

On the return of the forces those who had scoffed at the
Colored Troops on the march out were silent.

Nearly all the wounded were brought off though we had not an Ambulance in the command. The negro soldiers preferred present suffering to being murdered at the hands of a cruel enemy. I saw one man riding with his arm off another shot through the lungs and another shot through both hips.

Such of the Colored Soldiers as fell into the hands of the Enemy during the battle were brutally murdered. The Negroes did not retaliate but treated the Rebel wounded with great kindness, carrying them water in their canteens and doing all they could to alleviate the sufferings of those whom the fortunes of war had placed in their hands.

Col. Wade handled his command with skill bravery and good judgement, evincing his capacity to command a much larger force. I am General Very Respectfully Your Obedt. Servant

HLS

James S Brisbin

୶

While black soldiers anxiously awaited each test of arms, their families contemplated the injury or death of a loved one. Apprehensive about her son's safety as well as her own survival, the elderly mother of a Pennsylvania soldier petitioned President Lincoln for his release from the army.

Carlisles [Pa.]   nov 21 1864

Mr abarham lincon   I wont to knw sir if you please wether I can have my son relest from the arme   he is all the subport I have now   his father is Dead and his brother that wase all

the help that I had   he has bean wonded twise   he has not
had nothing to send me yet   now I am old and my head is
blossaming for the grave and if you dou I hope the lord will
bless you and me   if you please answer as soon as you can
if you please   tha say that you will simpethise withe the
poor   thear wase awhite jentel man told me to write to
you   Mrs jane Welcom if you please answer it to
  he be long to the eight rigmat co a u st colard
troops   mart welcom is his name   he is a sarjent
AL   [*Jane Welcome*]

President Lincoln forwarded Welcome's letter to the Bureau
of Colored Troops, which informed her that "the interests of
the service will not permit that your request be granted."[20]

The enlistment of black soldiers did not always entail sepa-
ration from their families. In Union-occupied parts of the
Confederacy, parents, wives, and children often lived in contraband camps near the soldiers' bivouacs, enjoying a measure of security by virtue of these arrangements. But in the
border states, where slavery remained in force, federal commanders refused food and protection to the families of black
soldiers, on the grounds that their owners were responsible
for their support. Many owners, however, repudiated the
obligation and drove away the soldiers' kinfolk to fend for
themselves. Joseph Miller, a soldier from Kentucky,
described the ordeal of his family.

[20] *Black Military Experience*, p. 665n.

Camp Nelson Ky   November 26, 1864
Personally appered before me E. B W Restieaux Capt. and
Asst. Quartermaster Joseph Miller a man of color who being
duly sworn upon oath says

I was a slave of George Miller of Lincoln County Ky.   I have
always resided in Kentucky and am now a Soldier in the
service of the United States.   I belong to Company I 124 U.S.C.
Inft now Stationed at Camp Nelson Ky.   When I came to
Camp for the purpose of enlisting about the middle of October
1864 my wife and children came with me because my master
said that if I enlisted he would not maintain them and I knew
they would be abused by him when I left.   I had then four
children ages respectively ten nine seven and four years.   On
my presenting myself as a recruit I was told by the Lieut. in
command to take my family into a tent within the limits of the
Camp.   My wife and family occupied this tent by the express
permission of the aforementioned Officer and never received
any notice to leave until Tuesday November 22" when a
mounted guard gave my wife notice that she and her children
must leave Camp before early morning.   This was about six
O'clock at night.   My little boy about seven years of age had
been very sick and was slowly recovering   My wife had no
place to go and so remained until morning.   About eight
Oclock Wednesday morning November 23" a mounted guard
came to my tent and ordered my wife and children out of
Camp   The morning was bitter cold.   It was freezing
hard.   I was certain that it would kill my sick child to take him
out in the cold.   I told the man in charge of the guard that it
would be the death of my boy   I told him that my wife and
children had no place to go and I told him that I was a soldier
of the United States.   He told me that it did not make any
difference.   he had orders to take all out of Camp.   He told
my wife and family that if they did not get up into the wagon

which he had he would shoot the last one of them.   On being
thus threatened my wife and children went into the
wagon   My wife carried her sick child in her arms.   When
they left the tent the wind was blowing hard and cold and
having had to leave much of our clothing when we left our
master, my wife with her little one was poorly clad.   I
followed them as far as the lines.   I had no Knowledge where
they were taking them.   At night I went in search of my
family.   I found them at Nicholasville about six miles from
Camp.   They were in an old meeting house belonging to the
colored people.   The building was very cold having only one
fire.   My wife and children could not get near the fire, because
of the number of colored people huddled together by the
soldiers.   I found my wife and children shivering with cold
and famished with hunger   They had not recieved a morsel
of food during the whole day.   My boy was dead.   He died
directly after getting down from the wagon.   I Know he was
Killed by exposure to the inclement weather   I had to return
to camp that night so I left my family in the meeting house and
walked back.   I had walked there.   I travelled in all twelve
miles   Next morning I walked to Nicholasville.   I dug a
grave myself and buried my own child.   I left my family in
the Meeting house—where they still remain   And further
this deponent saith not

his

HDcSr   (Signed)   Joseph   Miller

mark

⌒⌒

When military duties took them far afield, soldiers chafed

at their inability to rescue their families from slavery. Joseph Harris, a sergeant from Louisiana who found himself stationed in distant Florida, turned for assistance to General Daniel Ullmann, who had supervised recruitment in his home state. Recounting his regiment's battlefield success, Sergeant Harris felt confident that the general would grant him "a Small favor."

Barrancas Fla.   Dec 27. 1864

Sir   I beg you the granterfurction of a Small favor   will you ples to Cross the Mississippia River at Bayou Sar La. with your Command & jest on the hill one mile from the little town you will finde A plantation Called Mrs Marther. H. Turnbuill & take a way my Farther & mother & my brothers wife with all their Childern & U take them up at your He^d Quarters. & write to me   Sir the ar ther & I will amejeately Send after them.   I wishes the Childern all in School.   it is beter for them then to be their Surveing a mistes.   Sir it isent mor then three or four Hours trubel   I have bain trying evry sence I have bin in the servis it is goin on ner 3. years & Could never get no one to so do for me   now I thinks it will be don for you is my Gen.   I wishes evry day you would send after us.   our Regt. ar doing all the hard fightin her   we have disapointe the Rebes & surprizeed theme in all. importan pointes   they says they wishes to Captuer the 82nd Regt that they woul murdar them all   they Calls our Reg^t the Bluebellied Eagles   Sir my Farthers Name Adam Harris   he will Call them all to gether. & tel him to take Cousan Janes Childarn with hime

Joseph. J. Harris

Sir I will remain Ob your Soldiar in the U.S.A.

ALS

During the waning months of the war, efforts to inaugurate political reconstruction prompted intense debate about slavery and freedom, loyalty and treason, and the rights of citizens. Active in that debate were Americans of African descent, who argued that their services to the nation had entitled them not only to freedom but also to civil and political rights. Black Tennesseans petitioned a convention of white unionists that had assembled to consider reorganizing the state government and abolishing slavery. To demonstrate the fitness of black men to vote and to exercise the other privileges of citizenship, the petitioners emphasized the role of black soldiers in saving the Union. In the months and years to come, this theme would reappear in countless demands by former slaves for full citizenship.

[*Nashville, Tenn., January 9, 1865*]
To the Union Convention of Tennessee Assembled in the Capitol at Nashville, January 9th, 1865:
We the undersigned petitioners, American citizens of African descent, natives and residents of Tennessee, and devoted friends of the great National cause, do most respectfully ask a patient hearing of your honorable body in regard to matters deeply affecting the future condition of our unfortunate and long suffering race.

First of all, however, we would say that words are too weak to tell how profoundly grateful we are to the Federal Government for the good work of freedom which it is gradually carrying forward; and for the Emancipation Proclamation which has set free all the slaves in some of the

Above and opposite: Letter from Sergeant Joseph J. Harris to General Daniel Ullmann (see p. 140).

I have bain trying every sence
I have him in the servis it is
goin an ner 3 years & could never
yet no one to Sode for me now
I thinks it will be don for you
is my Genl. I wishes every day
you would send after us. our
Regt. as doing all the hard fighter
in her we have disapointe the Rebes
& Surprizeed theme in all importan
pointes they says they wishes to
Capture the 82nd Regt that they
woul murder them all they calls
our Regt the Bluebellied Eagles
Sir My Brothers Name Adam Harn
he will call them all to gether
& tel him to take Cousan Jane's
Childarn with him

Jeseph Jno Harris 1th Sgt. E. Co.

Sir I will remain Oble
your Soldier in the U. S. A.

Proclamation which has set free all the slaves in some of the rebellious States, as well as many of the slaves in Tennessee.[21]

After two hundred years of bondage and suffering a returning sense of justice has awakened the great body of the American people to make amends for the unprovoked wrongs committed against us for over two hundred years.

Your petitioners would ask you to complete the work begun by the nation at large, and abolish the last vestige of slavery by the express words of your organic law.

Many masters in Tennessee whose slaves have left them, will certainly make every effort to bring them back to bondage after the reorganization of the State government, unless slavery be expressly abolished by the Constitution.

We hold that freedom is the natural right of all men, which they themselves have no more right to give or barter away, than they have to sell their honor, their wives, or their children.

We claim to be men belonging to the great human family, descended from one great God, who is the common Father of all, and who bestowed on all races and tribes the priceless right of freedom.   Of this right, for no offence of ours, we have long been cruelly deprived, and the common voice of the wise and good of all countries, has remonstrated against our enslavement, as one of the greatest crimes in all history.

We claim freedom, as our natural right, and ask that in harmony and co-operation with the nation at large, you should cut up by the roots the system of slavery, which is not only a wrong to us, but the source of all the evil which at present afflicts the State.   For slavery, corrupt itself, corrupted nearly all, also, around it, so that it has influenced nearly all the slave States to rebel against the Federal

---

[21] The Emancipation Proclamation of January 1, 1863, exempted the state of Tennessee from its provisions. (*Statutes at Large*, vol. 12, pp. 1268–69.)

Government, in order to set up a government of pirates under which slavery might be perpetrated.

In the contest between the nation and slavery, our unfortunate people have sided, by instinct, with the former. We have little fortune to devote to the national cause, for a hard fate has hitherto forced us to live in poverty, but we do devote to its success, our hopes, our toils, our whole heart, our sacred honor, and our lives. We will work, pray, live, and, if need be, die for the Union, as cheerfully as ever a white patriot died for his country. The color of our skin does not lesson in the least degree, our love either for God or for the land of our birth.

We are proud to point your honorable body to the fact, that so far as our knowledge extends, not a negro traitor has made his appearance since the beginning of this wicked rebellion.

Whether freeman or slaves the colored race in this country have always looked upon the United States as the Promised Land of Universal freedom, and no earthly temptation has been strong enough to induce us to rebel against it. We love the Union by an instinct which is stronger than any argument or appeal which can be used against it. It is the attachment of a child to its parent.

Devoted as we are to the principles of justice, of love to all men, and of equal rights on which our Government is based, and which make it the hope of the world. We know the burdens of citizenship, and are ready to bear them. We know the duties of the good citizen, and are ready to perform them cheerfully, and would ask to be put in a position in which we can discharge them more effectually. We do not ask for the privilege of citizenship, wishing to shun the obligations imposed by it.

Near 200,000 of our brethren are to-day performing military duty in the ranks of the Union army. Thousands of them have already died in battle, or perished by a cruel martyrdom for the sake of the Union, and we are ready and willing to sacrifice more.   But what higher order of citizen is there than the soldier?   or who has a greater trust confided to his hands?   If we are called on to do military duty against the rebel armies in the field, why should we be denied the privilege of voting against rebel citizens at the ballot-box?   The latter is as necessary to save the Government as the former.

. . . .

This is a democracy—a government of the people.   It should aim to make every man, without regard to the color of his skin, the amount of his wealth, or the character of his religious faith, feel personally interested in its welfare.   Every man who lives under the Government should feel that it is his property, his treasure, the bulwark and defence of himself and his family, his pearl of great price, which he must preserve, protect, and defend faithfully at all times, on all occasions, in every possible manner.

This is not a Democratic Government if a numerous, law-abiding, industrious, and useful class of citizens, born and bred on the soil, are to be treated as aliens and enemies, as an inferior degraded class, who must have no voice in the Government which they support, protect and defend, with all their heart, soul, mind, and body, both in peace and war.

This Government is based on the teachings of the Bible, which prescribes the same rules of action for all members of the human family, whether their complexion be white, yellow, red or black.   God no where in his revealed word, makes an invidious and degrading distinction against his children, because of their color.   And happy is that nation which makes the Bible its rule of action, and obeys principle, not prejudice.

Let no man oppose this doctrine because it is opposed to his old prejudices.   The nation is fighting for its life, and cannot afford to be controlled by prejudice. Had prejudice prevailed instead of principle, not a single colored soldier would have been in the Union army to-day. But principle and justice triumphed, and now near 200,000 colored patriots stand under the folds of the national flag, and brave their breasts to the bullets of the rebels. As we are in the battlefield, so we swear before heaven, by all that is dear to men, to be at the ballot-box faithful and true to the Union.

The possibility that the negro suffrage proposition may shock popular prejudice at first sight, is not a conclusive argument against its wisdom and policy. No proposition ever met with more furious or general opposition than the one to enlist colored soldiers in the United States army. The opponents of the measure exclaimed on all hands that the negro was a coward; that he would not fight; that one white man, with a whip in his hand could put to flight a regiment of them; that the experiment would end in the utter rout and ruin of the Federal army. Yet the colored man has fought so well, on almost every occasion, that the rebel government is prevented, only by its fears and distrust of being able to force him to fight for slavery as well as he fights against it, from putting half a million of negroes into its ranks.

The Government has asked the colored man to fight for its preservation and gladly has he done it. It can afford to trust him with a vote as safely as it trusted him with a bayonet.

. . . .

In this great and fearful struggle of the nation with a wicked rebellion, we are anxious to perform the full measure of our duty both as citizens and soldiers   to the Union cause we consecrate ourselves, and our families, with all that we have on earth. Our souls burn with love for the great government of freedom and equal rights. Our white brethren have no cause for distrust as regards our fidelity, for neither death nor life, nor angels, nor principalities, nor powers, nor things present, nor things to come, nor height, nor depth, nor any other creature, shall be able to separate us from the love of the Union.

Praying that the great God, who is the common Father of us all, by whose help the land must be delivered from present evil, and before whom we must all stand at last to be judged by the rule of eternal justice, and not by passion and prejudice, may enlighten your minds and enable you to act with wisdom, justice, and magnanimity, we remain your faithful friends in all the perils and dangers which threaten our beloved country.

[59 signatures]

PDSr   And many other colored citizens of Nashville

The convention adopted an amendment to the state constitution abolishing slavery, which was ratified on February 22, 1865. The delegates took no action to extend the rights of citizenship to black Tennesseans.

∾

In Savannah, Georgia, on the evening of January 12, 1865, assembled one of the most remarkable gatherings of the Civil War era. Twenty black ministers and lay leaders joined Secretary of War Edwin M. Stanton and General William T. Sherman at the general's headquarters. They had been summoned to consider the future of the thousands of slaves freed by the scourging march of Sherman's army. The Reverend Garrison Frazier, a sixty-seven-year-old ex-slave who had purchased his freedom before the war, served as spokesman. A Northern newspaper reported the proceedings.

[*New York, N.Y.   February 13, 1865*]
· · · ·

MINUTES OF AN INTERVIEW BETWEEN THE COLORED MINISTERS
AND CHURCH OFFICERS AT SAVANNAH WITH THE SECRETARY OF
WAR AND MAJOR-GEN. SHERMAN.
HEADQUARTERS OF MAJ.-GEN. SHERMAN, ⎫
CITY OF SAVANNAH, GA., Jan., 12, 1865—8 P.M. ⎬
· · · ·   ⎭

Garrison Frazier being chosen by the persons present to
express their common sentiments upon the matters of
inquiry, makes answers to inquiries as follows:

First: State what your understanding is in regard to the
acts of Congress and President Lincoln's [*Emancipation*]
proclamation, touching the condition of the colored people in
the Rebel States.

Answer—So far as I understand President Lincoln's
proclamation to the Rebellious States, it is, that if they would
lay down their arms and submit to the laws of the United
States before the first of January, 1863, all should be well; but
if they did not, then all the slaves in the Rebel States should
be free henceforth and forever.   That is what I understood.

Second—State what you understand by Slavery and the
freedom that was to be given by the President's proclamation.

Answer—Slavery is, receiving by *irresistible power* the work
of another man, and not by his *consent*.   The freedom, as I
understand it, promised by the proclamation, is taking us
from under the yoke of bondage, and placing us where we
could reap the fruit of our own labor, take care of ourselves
and assist the Government in maintaining our freedom.

Third: State in what manner you think you can take care
of yourselves, and how can you best assist the Government in
maintaining your freedom.

Answer: The way we can best take care of ourselves is to
have land, and turn it and till it by our own labor—that is, by

the labor of the women and children and old men; and we can soon maintain ourselves and have something to spare.   And to assist the Government, the young men should enlist in the service of the Government, and serve in such manner as they may be wanted.   (The Rebels told us that they piled them up and made batteries of them, and sold them to Cuba; but we don't believe that.)   We want to be placed on land until we are able to buy it and make it our own.

Fourth: State in what manner you would rather live— whether scattered among the whites or in colonies by yourselves.

Answer: I would prefer to live by ourselves, for there is a prejudice against us in the South that will take years to get over; but I do not know that I can answer for my brethren.   [Mr. Lynch says he thinks they should not be separated, but live together.   All the other persons present, being questioned one by one, answer that they agree with Brother Frazier.]22

Fifth: Do you think that there is intelligence enough among the slaves of the South to maintain themselves under the Government of the United States and the equal protection of its laws, and maintain good and peaceable relations among yourselves and with your neighbors?

Answer—I think there is sufficient intelligence among us to do so.

Sixth—State what is the feeling of the black population of the South toward the Government of the United States; what is the understanding in respect to the present war—its causes and object, and their disposition to aid either side.   State fully your views.

Answer—I think you will find there are thousands that are

---

22 Brackets in the original. The "Mr. Lynch" who dissented from the views of Garrison Frazier and the other black leaders was James Lynch, a Northern missionary sponsored by the African Methodist Episcopal Church.

willing to make any sacrifice to assist the Government of the United States, while there are also many that are not willing to take up arms.   I do not suppose there are a dozen men that are opposed to the Government.   I understand, as to the war, that the South is the aggressor.   President Lincoln was elected President by a majority of the United States, which guaranteed him the right of holding the office and exercising that right over the whole United States.   The South, without knowing what he would do, rebelled.   The war was commenced by the Rebels before he came into office.   The object of the war was not at first to give the slaves their freedom, but the sole object of the war was at first to bring the rebellious States back into the Union and their loyalty to the laws of the United States.   Afterward, knowing the value set on the slaves by the Rebels, the President thought that his proclamation would stimulate them to lay down their arms, reduce them to obedience, and help to bring back the Rebel States; and their not doing so has now made the freedom of the slaves a part of the war.   It is my opinion that there is not a man in this city that could be started to help the Rebels one inch, for that would be suicide.   There were two black men left with the Rebels because they had taken an active part for the Rebels, and thought something might befall them if they stayed behind; but there is not another man.   If the prayers that have gone up for the Union army could be read out, you would not get through them these two weeks.

Seventh: State whether the sentiments you now express are those only of the colored people in the city; or do they extend to the colored population through the country? and what are your means of knowing the sentiments of those living in the country?

Answer: I think the sentiments are the same among the colored people of the State.   My opinion is formed by personal communication in the course of my ministry, and also from the thousands that followed the Union army, leaving their homes and undergoing suffering. I did not think there would be so many; the number surpassed my expectation.

Eighth: If the Rebel leaders were to arm the slaves, what would be its effect?

Answer: I think they would fight as long as they were before the bayonet, and just as soon as soon as they could get away, they would desert, in my opinion.

Ninth: What, in your opinion, is the feeling of the colored people about enlisting and serving as soldiers of the United States? and what kind of military service do they prefer?

Answer: A large number have gone as soldiers to Port Royal [S.C.] to be drilled and put in the service; and I think there are thousands of the young men that would enlist. There is something about them that perhaps is wrong. They have suffered so long from the Rebels that they want to shoulder the musket. Others want to go into the Quartermaster's or Commissary's service.

Tenth: Do you understand the mode of enlistments of colored persons in the Rebel States by State agents under the Act of Congress?[23] If yea, state what your understanding is.

Answer: My understanding is, that colored persons enlisted by State agents are enlisted as substitutes, and give credit to the States, and do not swell the army, because every black man enlisted by a State agent leaves a white man at home; and, also, that larger bounties are given or promised by State agents than are given by the States. The great object should be to push through this Rebellion the shortest way, and there seems to be something wanting in the enlistment by State agents, for it don't strengthen the army, but takes one away for every colored man enlisted.

---

[23] A law adopted in July 1864 permitted agents from Northern states to recruit soldiers among black men in the Confederate states, crediting them against the draft quotas of the Northern states. (*Statutes at Large*, vol. 13, pp. 379–81.)

Eleventh: State what, in your opinion, is the best way to enlist colored men for soldiers.

Answer: I think, sir, that all compulsory operations should be put a stop to.   The ministers would talk to them, and the young men would enlist.   It is my opinion that it would be far better for the State agents to stay at home, and the enlistments to be made for the United States under the direction of Gen. Sherman.

In the absence of Gen. Sherman, the following question was asked:

Twelfth: State what is the feeling of the colored people in regard to Gen. Sherman; and how far do they regard his sentiments and actions as friendly to their rights and interests, or otherwise?

Answer: We looked upon Gen. Sherman prior to his arrival as a man in the Providence of God specially set apart to accomplish this work, and we unanimously feel inexpressible gratitude to him, looking upon him as a man that should be honored for the faithful performance of his duty.   Some of us called upon him immediately upon his arrival, and it is probable he would not meet the Secretary with more courtesy than he met us.   His conduct and deportment toward us characterized him as a friend and a gentleman.   We have confidence in Gen. Sherman, and think that what concerns us could not be under better hands.   This is our opinion now from the short acquaintance and interest we have had.   (Mr. Lynch states that with his limited acquaintance with Gen. Sherman, he is unwilling to express an opinion.   All others present declare their agreement with Mr. Frazier about Gen. Sherman.)

Some conversation upon general subjects relating to Gen. Sherman's march then ensued, of which no note was taken.

. . . .

PD

As more and more of the Confederacy came under Union
control, liberated slaves explored the new possibilities
opened by their war-born emancipation. Among these was
the opportunity to obtain legal marriages and thereby
affirm the integrity of their families, which, under slavery,
had always been at risk. In a report to the adjutant general
of the army, the chaplain of a black regiment in Arkansas
confirmed the importance of marriage to soldiers and other
freedpeople, and described their conviction that emancipation was less an end than a beginning.

Little Rock   Ark   Feb 28th 1865
The movements of the 54th during the month has interfered
to some extent with our Sabbath services; and has also,
rendered it impracticable to continue the day school.   On
reaching this post from, Ft Smith, the Regt was divided, and
five companies sent out towards Brownsville, to guard the
Rail Road.   These have been ordered back to Little Rock and
the ten companies, are now camped, on the north side of the
river, doing guard, & provost, duty in & around Little
Rock: As soon as a building can be procured, I design to
open a day school for such as are disposed to attend.
    Weddings, just now, are very popular, and abundant
among the Colored People.   They have just learned, of the
Special Order No' 15. of Gen Thomas[24] by which, they may
not only be lawfully married, but have their Marriage

---

[24] Adjutant General Lorenzo Thomas's order authorized "[a]ny ordained minister of
the Gospel, accredited by the General Superintendent of Freedmen, . . . to solemnize
the rites of marriage among the Freedmen." (*Black Military Experience*, p. 712n.)

Certificates, *Recorded;* in a *book furnished by the Government.* This is most desirable; and the order, was very opportune; as these people were constantly loosing their certificates. Those who were captured from the "Chepewa"; at Ivy's Ford, on the 17ᵗʰ of January, by Col Brooks, had their Marriage Certificates, taken from them; and destroyed; and then were roundly cursed, for having such papers in their posession. I have married, during the month, at this Post; Twenty five couples; mostly, those, who have families; & have been living together for years. I try to dissuade single men, who are soldiers, from marrying, till their time of enlistment is out: as that course seems to me, to be most judicious.

The Colord People here, generally consider, this war not only; their *exodus,* from bondage; but the road, to Responsibility; Competency; and an honorable Citizenship— God grant that their hopes and expectations may be fully realized. Most Respectfully

ALS   A. B. Randall

∽

Slaveholders experienced the war as a passage to Hell rather than the road to a Promised Land. As slavery disintegrated, they grew increasingly bitter, often lashing out at those men, women, and children who remained under their control. None exceeded the fury of owners in loyal Kentucky, where nearly 60 percent of the black men of military age seized freedom by enlisting in the Union army, the largest proportion of any slave state. With the men beyond reach, the soldiers' families became targets of the slaveholders' ire.

Patsey Leach, whose husband had died in combat, testified
to the consequences of her master's rage.

                        Camp Nelson   Ky   25" March 1865
    Personally appeared before me J M Kelley Notary Public in
and for the County of Jessamine State of Kentucky Patsey
Leach a woman of color who being duly sworn according to
law doth depose and say—
    I am a widow and belonged to Warren Wiley of Woodford
County Ky.   My husband Julius Leach was a member of Co.
D. 5" U.S.C. Cavalry and was killed at the Salt Works Va.
about six months ago.   When he enlisted sometime in the fall
of 1864 he belonged to Sarah Martin Scott County Ky.   He
had only been about a month in the service when he was
killed.   I was living with aforesaid Wiley when he died.   He
knew of my husbands enlisting before I did but never said
any thing to me about it.   From that time he treated me more
cruelly than ever whipping me frequently without any cause
and insulting me on every occasion.   About three weeks
after my husband enlisted a Company of Colored Soldiers
passed our house and I was there in the garden and looked at
them as they passed.   My master had been watching me and
when the soldiers had gone I went into the kitchen.   My
master followed me and Knocked me to the floor senseless
saying as he did so, "You have been looking at them darned
Nigger Soldiers"   When I recovered my senses he beat me
with a cowhide   When my husband was Killed my master
whipped me severely saying my husband had gone into the
army to fight against white folks and he my master would let
me know that I was foolish to let my husband go he would
"take it out of my back," he would "Kill me by picemeal" and
he hoped "that the last one of the nigger soldiers would be
Killed"   He whipped me twice after that using similar

expressions   The last whipping he gave me he took me into the Kitchen tied my hands tore all my clothes off until I was entirely naked, bent me down, placed my head between his Knees, then whipped me most unmercifully until my back was lacerated all over, the blood oozing out in several places so that I could not wear my underclothes without their becoming saturated with blood.   The marks are still visible on my back.   On this and other occasions my master whipped me for no other cause than my husband having enlisted.   When he had whipped me he said "never mind God dam you when I am done with you tomorrow you never will live no more."   I knew he would carry out his threats so that night about 10 o'clock I took my babe and travelled to Arnolds Depot where I took the Cars to Lexington   I have five children,   I left them all with my master except the youngest and I want to get them but I dare not go near my master knowing he would whip me again.   My master is a Rebel Sympathizer and often sends Boxes of Goods to Rebel prisoners.   And further Deponent saith not.

Her

HDcSr   Signed   Patsey   Leach

mark

∾

With the war's end, federal authorities began rapidly demo- bilizing veteran regiments. As a result, black soldiers, whose terms of enlistment had begun later than those of most white soldiers, represented a larger proportion of the post- war army of occupation than they had of the wartime force. In the spring of 1865, at the time of the Confederate surren- der, black men accounted for approximately 11 percent of

Union soldiers; by the following fall, they made up 36 percent of the total.[25] As they took up positions in the defeated South, black soldiers found themselves in close contact with civilians, black and white, and they assumed special responsibility for protecting the lives and liberty of the freedpeople among whom they were stationed. A sergeant from Michigan complained to the military commander in South Carolina when a post commander failed to render justice to a freedman who had appealed to him.

Columbia S.C   August 7th /65

Dear Sir   With Due Respect to you, after Coming to this pleasant City and Getting somewhat acquainted I find the freedmen are Shamefuly abused   for instance one Andrew Lee a Collord man Come in from the Country to Report some White men for Going into his house and Breaking open his trunks with a pretinse of searching for a hog that they Claimed to have lost.   The Said Andrew Lee Went General Horton Commanding Post and Entered Complaint   after hearing Andrew Lees Complaint he General Horton told Lee to Go off and that he General Horton had ought to put Lee in the Guard house and that those men had a Wright to search his house   This is a queer state of things Brought about to allow those Miscreants to plunder houses Without Some officer or Written authority   Sir I am only a sergeant and of Course Should be as silent as posible But in this I Could not hold my temper After fighting to get wrights that White men might Respect By Virtue of the Law   Sir I Would further say to you try and Give those things Due Considderation   No More But Remain Yours With Respect and true friend to the Union

ALS   E S Robison

---

[25] *Black Military Experience*, p. 733.

While service in the postwar army enabled black soldiers to assist nearby freedpeople, it also separated them from their own families, many of whom suffered from privation and abuse, and some of whom were still held in bondage. With the Confederate enemy vanquished, black soldiers petitioned to be mustered out so they might provide for their kin. On behalf of comrades from Missouri and Tennessee, an anonymous black soldier outlined to the secretary of war the men's concern about their families, as well as their dissatisfaction with routine duties and an obnoxious officer.

Chattanooga Ten.   August th 22 1865

Sir   I have the honor of Reporting Sevral condishtion to you about difference Circumstance   the Colored Men of these 44th & 16th & 18th there Wives is Scatered abut over world without pertioction in Suffernce condishtion & there Husband is here & have not seen there Faimlys for 2 years & more   we would be under ten thousand obligations to you if pervid Some plain for Our benfit   the greats Duites that is performed at this Place is Poleasing Ground   Some of us has not heard from our Wivies for 2 & a half [*years*] & Some of theses Familys I am very sure that is worse then I Repersent them to be   the all says the would be willing to fight there Enemy but at the present time is no fighting on this side of the Rior Grand   the says that dont want to go their whilce thire Familys is in a Suffernce condishtion but to Fight in the U.S.A. the all say the will do it without Truble   the think under the present [*circumstances*] of their Familys the ought to be permitt to go & see after Familys   I was late from Mo. & Ka. & anomber of them that I saw all most Thread less &

Shoeless without food & no home to go   sevral of there
Masters Run them off & as fur as I can see the hole Race will
fall back if the U.S. Goverment dont pervid for them Some
way or ruther   the is noumbers of them here at this place
suffering for the want of Husband Care   the Ration is
giving to them dose not degree very well with
Childern   recording to there Enlistments there times is out
for the war is over   the Enlist 3 years or during [*the*
war]   well the war is over   the is some talk of
consolidating Regiments   Some of the Officers says if the
men will Stack ther Arms[26] the will Stand at the head of there
Companys until the fall   I glorys in there Spunk   I am a
friend to the U.S. Goverment but [*not*] to Col. L. Johnson of
the 44th U.S.C.I   please reply to this   Col Johnson if he
Don't look out he will git apple cart tumbled   he has been
kicking some of the Boys but the say the will stop that or stop
his life & I am will to report the case before hand   I am very
respectful and & &

these three Regiments that I Speak of has a very notion to
Stack there Armys because there times of Enliting is
out   the say the Enlited 3 years or during the War & the war
is over & there times is out.
HL

∾

Black soldiers looked forward to their discharge as both a
time to reunite with loved ones and an opportunity to build

---

[26] Stacking arms signified collective refusal to perform duties and was tantamount to
mutiny.

a new world on the ashes of the old. Individual efforts at self-improvement and group efforts at self-help depended to large extent, they realized, on the skills of literacy. Writing to an official of the Freedmen's Bureau, a federal agency established in March 1865 to oversee the transition from slavery to freedom, a sergeant from Kentucky emphasized the importance of education to his people.

Nashville Tenn   October 8th 1865
Sir   I have the honor to call your attention To the neccesity of having a school for The benefit of our regement   We have never Had an institutiong of that sort and we Stand deeply inneed of instruction the majority of us having been slaves   We Wish to have some benefit of education To make of ourselves capable of buisness In the future   We have estableshed a literary Association which flourished previous to our March to Nashville   We wish to become a People capable of self support as we are Capable of being soldiers   my home is in Kentucky Where Prejudice reigns like the Mountain Oak and I do lack that cultivation of mind that would have an attendency To cast a cloud over my future life after have been in the United States service   I had a leave of abscence a few weeks a go on A furlough and it made my heart ache to see my race of people there neglected And ill treated on the account of the lack of Education being incapable of putting Thier complaints or applications in writing   For the want of Education totally ignorant Of the Great Good Workings of the Government in our behalf   We as soldiers Have our officers Who are our protection To teach how us to act and to do   But Sir What we want is a general system of education In our regiment for our moral and literary elevation   these being our motives We have the

Honor of calling your very high Consideration
Respectfully Submitted as Your Most humble serv^t
ALS   John Sweeny

Sweeny's request fell on receptive ears. The letter is endorsed:
"Will send Teacher as soon as possible."[27]

∽

Black soldiers demonstrated an interest in education not
only within their own ranks, but also in the communities
where they served. When former slaves in a northeastern
Mississippi town sought to establish a school, they enlisted
the aid of two noncommissioned officers.

Okolona Miss   Oct 25 1865,
Regtl Orders No 137   Sergt Eli Helen and Corporal Joseph
Ingram Co K having been selected by the Colored Citizens of
Okolona and vicinity as collecting agents for the fund to
establish a school for colored children, are hereby granted
permission to visit Okolona in the execution of their duties as
such
    This order to continue in force during their good behavior
By order of Col John S Bishop
HD

[27] *Black Military Experience*, p. 615n.

First page of letter from Sergeant John Sweeny to General Clinton B. Fisk
(see p. 161).

Former slaveholders despised black soldiers for the same reasons former slaves esteemed them. To men and women who had owned slaves, armed black men in positions of authority embodied the world turned upside down. Soldiers defending freedpeople or even advising them of their rights appeared to former slaveholders as dangerous provocateurs. A Mississippi planter warned three state legislators that disaster loomed unless the "Negro Soldiery" was removed.

Panola [*Miss.*].   Oct 22ᵈ, 1865

Gentlemen.   I wish to call your attention to a serious & growing evil, with the hope that you will give it your earliest attention, that something may be done to remove it from our midst—   The Negro Soldiery here are constantly telling our negroes, that for the next year, The Goverment will give them lands, provisions, Stock & all things necessary to carry on business for themselves,—& are constantly advising them not to make contracts with white persons, for the next year.—   Strange to say the negroes believe such stories in spite of facts to the contrary told them by their ~~masters~~ employers.—   The consequence is they are becoming careless, & impudent more & more, for they are told by the soldiers that they are as good as the whites & that they have come here for their protection & that they shall not be hurt.—   furthermore I have good cause to believe that our negroes are told that when the soldiers are withdrawn, that the whites will endeavor to enslave them again—& that they are urged to begin at an early day, perhaps about Christmas, a massacre of the whites, in order to ensure their freedom, & that if the whites are got out the way here, that then they will have no further apprehension—& that this Country will then be given to them by the northern people forever as an inheritance.—& Gentlemen to ignorant persons situated as the negro is such arguments seem quite plausible.— In truth the people of the South are in very great danger, more so than many suppose— I have been born & reared in the midst of negroes. I know their nature well, & have never, yet been deceived in my estimate of them. I am no alarmist, but I tell you most seriously that the whole south is resting upon a volcano—& that if the negro troops are not removed from our mids pretty Soon—that trouble of the direst kind will befal us— They will stimulate the negroes to insurrection & will then lend them a helping hand— It is well Known here that our negroes through the country are well supplied with fire arms, muskets, Double Barrel, shot Guns & Pistols,—& furthermore, it would be well if they are free to prohibit the use of fire arms until they had proved themselves to be good citizens in their altered state.— Gentlemen I do not write you these views hastily.— I have well considered them, & they appear more & more convincing day by day— I have talked with many of our citizens upon this matter— they appear anxious & say something ought to be done—but no one feels disposed to move in the matter.— Get the negro Soldiery removed from our midst & no danger will follow—our negroes will be quiet, will hire for another year.—& will do their duty in many cases very well— Let the Soldiery remain—& our negroes will refuse to hire will grow more & more insolent & will without a doubt—(relying upon the help of the Soldiery which they will be sure to get) will endeavor by universal Massacre to turn this fair land into another Hayti.[28]— Our

---

[28] In 1791, slaves in the French colony of Saint-Domingue revolted against their owners, killing or exiling all of them, and eventually establishing an independent republic (Haiti).

only hope of escape from the evils above enumerated &
many others, is to get the negro troops removed from the
State.   Cannot it be done?—   I think with Such men as Gov
Sharkey—& others like him making application to the
President to that effect, that the South can be Saved from
Anarchy & bloodshed—   Please to enlist youselves with Dr
Mosely in this matter, for much indeed depends upon it for
the weal or woe of our selves our wives & our little ones—
I remain Your friend, truly &c

                                                                E. G. Baker

P.S.   Esq Ballard has just told me that a squad of colored
Soldiers met him near his house this morning & without any
provocation—his not even speaking a word—they called him
a damned old rebel & threatened to kill, him; they did the
same to Wiley Baker a few minutes before using the most
vulgar abusive language to him—   they have several times
arrested citizens walking about the streets of a night
attending to their own business—their camp being down
near the old mill,—   they are generally drunk when they act
So—but the Lt who commands them when complained to
merely says that he does not authorise them to do so & there
the matter ends—   they are also killing up the hogs robbing
potatoe, patches,—parading (mustering) up & down the
streets in the most offensive manner.—   If things go on this
way much longer there will be a collison between the citizens
& the black rascals let the consequences be what they may—
Please to give the matter of their removal from our midst
your earliest & most serious attention—& you will have the
most lastings feelings of gratitude for your efforts in behalf of
the whole country—   Your friend— B.
ALS

Transmitting Baker's letter to the Union commander in
Northern Mississippi, Governor Benjamin G. Humphreys

advised that "unless some measures are taken to disarm [the freedmen] a collision between the races may be speedily looked for. . . . That the colored troops are the cause of the mischief is not doubted."[29]

∽

The ex-slaves' enemies in Mississippi were already taking steps to disarm them and further restrict their freedom. In late 1865, the state legislature enacted laws that acknowledged emancipation but severely limited the former slaves' liberty and legal rights. Meanwhile, ex-Confederates terrorized freedpeople under the pretext of averting a rumored insurrection. Hampered by a shortage of troops, the Mississippi branch of the Freedmen's Bureau under Colonel Samuel Thomas could barely begin to respond. In a letter to the bureau's national commissioner, a black private assigned to Thomas's office described the freedpeople's predicament and proposed a solution.

Vicksburg. Miss.   Dec 16th 1865.
Sir   Suffer me to address you a few lines in reguard to the colered people in this State,   from all I can learn and see, I think the colered people are in a great many ways being outraged beyound humanity,   houses have been tourn down from over the heades of women and Children—and the old Negroes after they have worked there till they are 70 or 80 yers of age drive them off in the cold to frieze and starve to death.

[29] *Black Military Experience*, p. 749n.

One Woman come to (Col) Thomas, the coldest day that
has been this winter and said that she and her eight children
lay out last night, and come near friezing after She had paid
some wrent on the house   Some are being knocked down
for saying they are free, while a great many are being worked
just as they ust to be when Slaves, without any
compensation,   Report came in town this morning that two
colered women was found dead side the Jackson road with
their throats cot lying side by side,   I see an account in the
Vicksburg. Journal where the (col[ored]) peple was having a
party where they formily had one. and got into a fuss and a
gun was fired and passed into a house.   they was forbidden
not to have any more but did not heed.   The result was the
house was fired and a guard placed at the door   one man
attemped to come out but was shot and throed back and
burned   five was consumed in the flames, while the balance
saught refuge in a church and it was fired and burned.   The
Rebbles are going a bout in many places through the State
and robbing the colered peple of arms money and all they
have and in many places killing.

So, General, to make short of a long story I think the safety
of this country depenes upon giving the Colered man all the
rights of a white man, and especialy the Rebs. and let him
know that their is power enough in the arm of the
Government to give Justice, to all her loyal citizens—

They talk of taking the armes a way from (col[ored]) people
and arresting them and put them on farmes next month[30]
and if they go at that I think there will be trouble and in all
probability a great many lives lost.   They have been

---

[30] A recently adopted state law required that all black men and women find a white
employer by the second week of January, failing which they would be arrested as
vagrants and forced to labor for whoever paid their fines.

accusing the colered peple of an insorection which is a lie, in order that they might get arms to carrie out their wicked designs—

for to my own knowledge I have seen them buying arms and munitions ever since the lins have been opened and carring them to the country.   In view of these things I would suggust to you if it is not incompatible with the public interest to pass some laws that will give protection to the colered men and meet out Justice to traters in arms.

For you have whiped them and tried them and found out that they will not do to be depended upon,   now if you have any true harted men send them down here to carrie out your wishes through the Bureau in reguarde to the freedmen.   if not get Congress to stick in a few competent colered men as they did in the army and the thing will all go right,   A trouble now with the colered peple on account of Rebs. after they have rendered the Government such great survice through the rebellion would spoil the whole thing—and it is what the Rebles would like to bring a bout, and they are doing all they can to prevent free labor, and reasstablish a kind of secondary slavery   Now believe me as a colered man that is a friend to law and order, I blive without the intervention of the General governmt in the protection of the (col[ored]) popble that there will be trouble in *Miss.* before spring   please excuse this for I could not have said less and done the subject Justice.   infact I could say more, but a hint to the wise is soficient   If you wish to drop me a line Direct Calvin. Holly. *Vick* Miss Box 2ᵈ   yours Most Respectfully,

ALS   Calvin. Holly., colered

As their postwar duties dragged on, soldiers who had been slaves increasingly likened military service to bondage. Hope of overcoming the hardships of the past seemed to fade with each passing day. Their long-suffering families were struggling against fearful adversity, reported members of a South Carolina regiment to the departmental commander. Moreover, as affordable land rapidly disappeared, they beheld the somber prospect of dependence on white Southerners who mocked their aspirations for freedom and independence.

Morris Island   So Ca   January 13 1866

My Dear Respictfully Friend General Sickels   it is with much Honor we take to write to you about the Circumstances of our case   now Genl do if you please Cir to this lookin to this [for us]. now General the Biggest Majority of our mens never had a Home Science this late wor Commence between the States   the Greatist majority of them had Runaway from they Rebels master & leave they wives & old mother & old Father & all they parent   jest Run away from they Rebels master in the years 1862. & 1863 & come Right in under the Bondage of Soldiers life living & according to agreement & promised we was expected to get out at the Closing of the wor, & then go back over the Rebels lands to look & seek for our wives & mother & Father

But General now to see that the wor is over & our Enlisment is out the Greatist majority of by two months & the General characters of our Regiment we do not think that the our Goverment have knowit   for Instant I think if he had know the General characters of our Regt he would let us go at the Closing of this [war]   for instant look & see that we never was freed yet   Run Right out of Slavery in to Soldiery & we hadent nothing atoll & our wifes & mother most all of them is aperishing all about where we leave them or abbout

First page of letter from men of the 33rd U.S. Colored Infantry to General
Daniel E. Sickles (see p. 170).

the Country & we hear on morris Island Perishing sometime
for something to Eate   Half of our money got to use up in
the Regtal Sutler for somthing to Eate & we all are
perrishing   our self & our Parent & wives all are Suffering

& do General if you Please do see & Enterceed & see if you
cannot do any good to get us out of this if you please
cir   for all other Colored Soldiers that had a Home & is well
situated at Home is go back but we that never had a Comford
Home we is heer yet & we will have to buy our lands &
places & by the time we get out of this all the Goverment
cheap. Property & all the lands that would be sold cheap will
be gone & we will have a Hard struggle to get along in the
U S   & then all the Southern white Peoples will have us for
alaughin & game after for our Braverist that we did to Run
away from them & come asoldiers   they will be glad to see
that we would not have but very little money & we would
not have any land, atoll for all the cheap in things are going
now   So do Gen you is the only one that we know could do
any good for us beside forwarded to Washington.   So Please
if you can do any good for us do it in the name of god   it is
a mejority of men of the 33 Regt USCT
HL

∾

Even after they had left the service and returned home,
black soldiers faced a formidable task in protecting themselves and their kin. The wife of a discharged soldier paid a
high price for his association with the Union army, as she
related to an agent of the Freedmen's Bureau.

[*Griffin, Ga.*]   Sept. 25, 1866
Rhoda Ann Childs came into this office and made the
following statement:

"Myself and husband were under contract with Mrs. Amelia Childs of Henry County, and worked from Jan. 1, 1866, until the crops were laid by, or in other words until the main work of the year was done, without difficulty. Then, (the fashion being prevalent among the planters) we were called upon one night, and my husband was demanded; I Said he was not there. They then asked where he was. I Said he was gone to the water mellon patch. They then Seized me and took me Some distance from the house, where they 'bucked' me down across a log, Stripped my clothes over my head, one of the men Standing astride my neck, and beat me across my posterior, two men holding my legs. In this manner I was beaten until they were tired. Then they turned me parallel with the log, laying my neck on a limb which projected from the log, and one man placing his foot upon my neck, beat me again on my hip and thigh. Then I was thrown upon the ground on my back, one of the men Stood upon my breast, while two others took hold of my feet and stretched My limbs as far apart as they could, while the man Standing upon my breast applied the Strap to my private parts until fatigued into stopping, and I was more dead than alive. Then a man, Supposed to be an ex-confederate Soldier, as he was on crutches, fell upon me and ravished me. During the whipping one of the men ran his pistol into me, and Said he had a hell of a mind to pull the trigger, and Swore they ought to Shoot me, as my husband had been in the 'God damned Yankee Army,' and Swore they meant to kill every black Son-of-a-bitch they could find that had ever fought against them. They then went back to the house, Seized my two daughters and beat them, demanding their father's pistol, and upon failure to get that, they entered the house and took Such articles of clothing as Suited their fancy, and decamped. There were concerned in this affair eight men, none of which could be recognized for certain.

her

HDSr   Roda Ann X Childs
                                                mark

∽

More than a year after the war ended, Kentucky soldiers stationed on the Mexican border compared their faithful service to the Union with the shoddy treatment they and their families had endured. With a sense of entitlement derived from the sacrifices of their "poor nation of colour" on behalf of the "great and noble cause," they challenged the commander-in-chief to make good the nation's promises to them.

White Ranch [*Tex.*]   July 3ʳᵈ 1866

Dear President   I have the honer to address the as followes   the few remarks i wish to say and to inform you of is this   the Condition of our familys in Kentucky and the Condition of our self   we Kentuckians are men that Came out in this great and noble cause   we did come out like men   we have stood up to geather with Comrades and have proved not only to the people but to the world that we have been faithfull and prompt to all dutys   we have fulfilled all posts that we have been put and then as for a Regiment Commander to treat the soldiers so mean as we have been treated i think it is out of the question   My President and vice i think as a dutyfull as the 116ᵗʰ Regiment of U.S. Coloured Infantry have not had no more quarters shown them then what as been i dont think it is right for i

think that there are not the tenth part of quarters shown us
that is intended for us for if our officers and field officers
would take the Law as it is given to them and use it they have
not the power to use such ill treatment   Mr President and
vice we learn by the papers that the sum of three Hundred
dollars that was promised us when we inlisted in the service
we would not get it   but if the Govener should turn out the
men of our standing barehanded i would like to know how
you would expect for us to live ear after   we are a nation
that was poor and had nothing when we came to the
service   we had neather house nor money no place to put
our familys   now these poor nation of colour have spent the
best part of his days in slavery   now then what must we
do   must we turn out to steal to get a start   we left our
wifes and Children no place for them to lay there heads   we
left them not counted on Eaqual footing as the white
people   they where looked on like dogs and we left them
with a willing mind to exicute our duty in the army of the
United States war to eather to make us a nation of people
eather in this generation or the next to come   now Mr
President i wish you to ansure this letter and let us know we
are to do as this Regiment is labouring under a great mistake
untill you let us know what we are to do and you will releive
our mind a great deal and we will remain your affectionate
Brother Soldier   Direct to

1est Sargint Wm White
1 "   Do   Mc Meail
2 "   Do   Taylor
[Corpor]arl Thomass

HLSr

Sources of Documents

Pages

84–87   [General David Hunter] to Edwin M. Stanton, 23 June 1862, *Black Military Experience*, pp. 50–53.

87–88   Samuel J. Kirkwood to General [Henry W. Halleck], 5 Aug. 1862, *Black Military Experience*, pp. 85–86.

89–91   Genl. in Chf. H. W. Halleck to Major Genl. U. S. Grant, 31 Mar. 1863, *Black Military Experience*, pp. 143–44.

91–92   John A. Andrew to George T. Downing, 23 Mar. 1863, *Black Military Experience*, pp. 88–89.

93–94   Adolph J. Gla et al. to Majr. Genl. N. P. Banks, 7 Apr. 1863, *Black Military Experience*, p. 329.

94–96   Capt. Elias D. Strunke to Brig. Genl. D. Ullman, 29 May 1863, *Black Military Experience*, pp. 528–29.

97–99   Brig. Genl. Elias S. Dennis to Colonel John A. Rawlins, 12 June 1863, *Black Military Experience*, pp. 532–34.

100–103 Testimony of Nathaniel Paige before the American Freedmen's Inquiry Commission, [Feb.? 1864], *Black Military Experience*, pp. 534–36.

103–4   O. G. Eiland to President Davis, 20 July 1863, *Black Military Experience*, pp. 284–85.

106–8   Hannah Johnson to Hon. Mr. Lincoln, 31 July 1863, *Black Military Experience*, pp. 582–83.

109–11   Statement of A Colored man, [Sept.? 1863], *Black Military Experience*, pp. 153–56.

112–13   Col. James C. Beecher to Brig. Genl. Edward A. Wild, 13 Sept. 1863, *Black Military Experience*, p. 493.

Pages

114–16   Corporal James Henry Gooding to Abraham Lincoln, 28 Sept. 1863, *Black Military Experience,* pp. 385–86.

117–18   Martha to My Dear Husband [Richard Glover], 30 Dec. 1863, *Black Military Experience,* p. 244.

118–20   Theodore Hodgkins to Hon. E. M. Stanton, 18 Apr. 1864, *Black Military Experience,* pp. 587–88.

121–22   Acting Chaplain Garland H. White to Hon. Wm. H. Seward, 18 May 1864, *Black Military Experience,* pp. 348–49.

122–24   Ruphus Wright to dear wife, 25 May 1864, *Black Military Experience,* p. 663.

124–25   Sergt. John F. Shorter et al. to the President of the United States, 16 July 1864, *Black Military Experience,* pp. 401–2.

126–28   Unsigned to My Dear Friend and x Pre., [Aug.] 1864, *Black Military Experience,* pp. 501–2.

128–29   G. H. Freeman to Madam, 19 Aug. 1864, *Black Military Experience,* pp. 600–601.

129–31   Brig. Gen. Edwd. A. Wild to Brig. Gen. G. F. Shepley, 1 Sept. 1864, *Destruction of Slavery,* pp. 98–99.

131–33   [Private Spotswood Rice] to My Children, [3 Sept. 1864], and Spotswood Rice to Kittey diggs, [3 Sept. 1864], *Black Military Experience,* pp. 689–90.

134–36   Col. James S. Brisbin to Brig. Gen. L. Thomas, 20 Oct. 1864, *Black Military Experience,* pp. 557–58.

136–37   [Jane Welcome] to abarham lincon, 21 Nov. 1864, *Black Military Experience,* p. 664.

138–39   Affidavit of Joseph Miller, 26 Nov. 1864, *Black Military Experience,* pp. 269–71.

140   1st Sgt. Joseph J. Harris to Gen. Ullman, 27 Dec. 1864, *Black Military Experience,* pp. 691–92.

141–48   Unidentified newspaper clipping of Andrew Tait et al. to the Union Convention of Tennessee, 9 Jan. 1865, *Black Military Experience,* pp. 811–16.

149–53   Clipping from *New-York Daily Tribune,* [13 Feb. 1865], *Wartime Genesis: Lower South,* pp. 332–37.

154–55   Chaplain A. B. Randall to Brig. Genl. L. Thomas, 28 Feb. 1865, *Black Military Experience,* p. 712.

Pages

156–57   Affidavit of Patsey Leach, 25 Mar. 1865, *Black Military Experience,* pp. 268–69.

158   Sergt. E. S. Robison to Major General Q. A. Gilmore, 7 Aug. 1865, *Black Military Experience,* p. 742.

159–60   Unsigned to Mr. E. M. Santon, 22 Aug. 1865, *Black Military Experience,* pp. 773–74.

161–62   1st Sergeant John Sweeny to Brigadier General Fisk, 8 Oct. 1865, *Black Military Experience,* p. 615.

162   Regtl. Orders No. 137, Head Quarters 108" U.S.C.I., 25 Oct. 1865, *Black Military Experience,* p. 749.

164–66   E. G. Baker to Messrs. Irby & Ellis & Mosely, 22 Oct. 1865, *Black Military Experience,* pp. 747–49.

167–69   Privt. Calvin Holly to Major General O. O. Howard, 16 Dec. 1865, *Black Military Experience,* pp. 754–56.

170–72   Unsigned to General Sickels, 13 Jan. 1866, *Black Military Experience,* pp. 777–78.

172–74   Affidavit of Roda Ann Childs, 25 Sept. 1866, *Black Military Experience,* p. 807.

174–75   Sargint Wm. White et al. to Dear President, 3 July 1866, *Black Military Experience,* pp. 763–64.

Suggestions for Further Reading

Of the vast literature on the U.S. Civil War, a small but growing proportion addresses the black military experience. This brief guide identifies the most important scholarly studies; those available in paperback are marked with an asterisk.

First to chronicle the story of black soldiers in the Civil War were men who had witnessed it at first hand. *The Negro in the American Rebellion: His Heroism and His Fidelity* (1867), by William Wells Brown, appeared just two years after the Confederate surrender. A former slave who had gained renown as an abolitionist orator, Brown celebrated black soldiers as saviors of the Union whose contributions had opened the door to full citizenship for Americans of African descent. By the late nineteenth century, when two black veterans published full-fledged histories, confidence that military service would receive its natural reward had begun to erode. George Washington Williams, *A History of the Negro Troops in the War of the Rebellion, 1861–1865* (1888), and Joseph T. Wilson, *The Black Phalanx: A History of the Negro Soldiers of the United States in the Wars of 1775–1812 and 1861–65* (1888), used government documents, observers' accounts, and the personal papers and recollections of participants to remind Americans of the heroism they and their comrades had exhibited, endeavoring thereby to counter the sectional rapprochement at the expense of black Americans.

A number of white officers who had commanded black soldiers also documented their men's service. In *Army Life in a Black Regi-

ment (1870), Thomas Wentworth Higginson, colonel of the 1st South Carolina Volunteers (33rd U.S. Colored Infantry), offers a series of vignettes about his encounter with the people and culture of the Carolina lowcountry. Luis F. Emilio, who became a lieutenant in the 54th Massachusetts Infantry at the age of eighteen, provides a detailed chronology of the regiment's service and invaluable biographies of the men who filled its ranks in *A Brave Black Regiment: The History of the Fifty-Fourth Regiment of Massachusetts Volunteer Infantry, 1863–1865,* 2nd ed. (1894). Emilio's regimental history is supplemented and enriched by *Blue-Eyed Child of Fortune: The Civil War Letters of Colonel Robert Gould Shaw* (1992), a collection of the letters of the commander of the 54th Massachusetts, edited by Russell Duncan. Also valuable is the diary of the commander of the 2nd Louisiana Native Guards (74th U.S. Colored Infantry), *Thank God My Regiment an African One: The Civil War Diary of Colonel Nathan W. Daniels* (1998), edited by C. P. Weaver.

Although those who commanded black soldiers knew them well, the men speak best for themselves. Historians have compiled several valuable collections. *On the Altar of Freedom: A Black Soldier's Civil War Letters from the Front, Corporal James Henry Gooding* (1991), edited by Virginia Matzke Adams, and *A Voice of Thunder: The Civil War Letters of George E. Stephens* (1997), edited by Donald Yacovone, offer letters written by two noncommissioned officers of the 54th Massachusetts for journals of the day. Although Gooding communicated with the white editors of the New Bedford (Mass.) *Mercury* and Stephens with the black editors of the New York *Weekly Anglo-African,* the two men present remarkably similar commentary on the soldiers' struggle for equality within Union ranks as well as their regiment's storied encounters with the Confederate foe.

Other collections of soldiers' letters—drawing from governmental archives as well as newspapers and other publications—paint composite pictures of the black military experience. James M. McPherson, ed., *The Negro's Civil War: How American Negroes Felt and Acted during the War for the Union* (1965), includes a broad sampling of opinion regarding issues raised by military service and in-depth treatment of the soldiers' world. Edwin R. Redkey, ed., *A Grand Army of Black Men: Letters from African-American Soldiers in the Union Army, 1861–1865* (1992), which draws on correspondence published in the *Weekly Anglo-African* and the A.M.E. *Christian Recorder,* documents the experiences of black men in the Union army and navy and illustrates their determination to destroy slavery and promote racial equality. Noah Andre Trudeau, ed., *Voices of the 55th: Letters from the 55th Massachusetts Volunteers, 1861–1865* (1996), captures the sentiments of men who stood in the shadow of the 54th Massachusetts yet faced comparable challenges.

Accounts by two women, one black and one white, cast light on the experiences of the 1st South Carolina Infantry. In *Reminiscences of My Life in Camp with the 33rd United States Colored Troops, Late 1st S.C. Volunteers* (1902), reprinted as *A Black Woman's Civil War Memoirs* (1988), Susie King Taylor, a former slave and the wife of an enlisted man, describes her labors as laundress, teacher, and nurse. *A Woman Doctor's Civil War: Esther Hill Hawks' Diary* (1984), edited by Gerald Schwartz, records the observations and experiences of the wife of the regiment's surgeon; herself a trained physician, she served as teacher, medical practitioner, and general benefactor of freedpeople in South Carolina's sea islands and in northeastern Florida.

Modern scholarly treatment of black soldiers in the Civil War dates from W. E. B. Du Bois, *Black Reconstruction: An Essay toward a History of the Part Which Black Folk Played in the Attempt to Reconstruct Democracy in America, 1860–1880* (1935). A pioneering study by Herbert Aptheker, *The Negro in the Civil War* (1938), provides an intellectual bridge between Du Bois's work and that of revisionist scholars writing after World War II. Several books by Benjamin Quarles, particularly *The Negro in the Civil War* (1953), describe the service of black soldiers and their impact on the war's outcome. In *The Sable Arm: Negro Troops in the Union Army, 1861–1865* (1966), Dudley Taylor Cornish demonstrates how the manuscript records at the National Archives supplement the War Department's official record. Leon F. Litwack's prize-winning study of emancipation, *Been in the Storm So Long: The Aftermath of Slavery* (1979), includes a chapter that summarizes and extends understanding of the black military experience.

A number of works published during the past decade draw upon the roadmap to the documentary record at the National Archives provided in *The Black Military Experience* (1982), edited by Ira Berlin, Joseph P. Reidy, and Leslie S. Rowland (series 2 of *Freedom: A Documentary History of Emancipation, 1861–1867*). Joseph T. Glatthaar, *Forged in Battle: The Civil War Alliance of Black Soldiers and White Officers* (1990), explores the troubled partnership between black soldiers and their white officers. Howard C. Westwood's collection of essays, *Black Troops, White Commanders, and Freedmen during the Civil War* (1992), considers the relationship of prominent political and military leaders to black recruitment and recounts dramatic incidents involving black troops. James G. Hollandsworth, Jr., *The Louisiana Native Guards: The Black Military Experience during the Civil War* (1995), narrates the service of the men—often freeborn and of mixed racial ancestry—who made up the Native Guard regiments. His study demonstrates the largely untapped possibility of combining local sources with the documentary record preserved at the National Archives to compile histories of individual regiments. Noah Andre Trudeau, *Like Men of War: Black Troops in the Civil War, 1862–1865* (1997), synthesizes eyewitness accounts and later commentaries to fashion a military history of black soldiers that discusses the most significant engagements in which they took part.

The new scholarship demonstrates both how much has been learned of freedom's soldiers and how much is yet to be known.

Index

Abolitionists: challenge Northern discrimination against blacks, 7; demand emancipation, 3; postwar activities of former white officers for black equality, 47; protest discrimination against black soldiers in Union army, 26, 45; recruit blacks for army, 12; tout military advantage of emancipation, 5; want black soldiers to be sent into battle, 37; worry whether blacks will fight effectively, vii

Alabama: number of blacks from in Union army, 20

Allen, Charles A.: letter from, 93–94

Allen, Colonel, 99

American Freedmen's Inquiry Commission: creation and purpose of, 10; testimony before concerning Fort Wagner, 100–102

Anderson, Captain, 97

Andrew, John A., 121; favors abolition and black enlistments, 8, 11, 13; favors commissioning black officers, 27, 28; letter from, 91–92; offers to supplement black soldiers' pay, 30

Army, Confederate: black experience in, 23; blacks would desert from, 152; Louisiana Native Guards serve in before arrival of federal troops, 92–93; opposition to slaves joining, 23; argument that slaves should be drafted into, 103–4; support for free black men enlisting, 23

Army, Union: 3rd New Hampshire, 102; 7th New Hampshire, 102; 10th Illinois Cavalry, 97; 11th Michigan Cavalry, 135; 12th Ohio Volunteer Cavalry, 134, 135; 23rd Iowa Volunteer Infantry, 97–99; seen as an army of liberation, 1; battle experience molds lives, 38; postwar demobilization of black regiments, 49,

157; discrimination against black soldiers in, 26, 32, 34, 35–36, 45, 46, 92, 109; needs more laborers, 18, 87, 88, 89; needs more soldiers, 10, 33, 36–37; number of black men in, vii, 20, 157–58; routine life in, 39; segregation of, 2, 25, 25n; use of slaves in justifies use of in Confederate army, 104; struggle for equality in, 40. See also Black regiments; Black soldiers

Baker, E. G.: letter from, 164–66

Baker, Wiley: threatened by black soldiers, 166

Ballad: broadside honoring black volunteers, 55

Ballard, Mr.: threatened by black soldiers, 166

Banks, Nathaniel P.: letter to, 93–94; as Massachusetts governor vetoes black militia service, 7; opposes black commissioned officers, 27, 93; command of near New Orleans, 89

Beecher, James C.: letter from, 112–13

Bible: principles of should rule, 146

Bishop, John S., 162

Black men: eager to fight, vii, 8, 94, 115; covet liberator role, 1; gain confidence from military service, 2; number of in North, 15; purpose of enlisting, 9, 21; want revenge against slaveholders, vii

Black people: bravery of, 110; discrimination within Union army causes distrust among, 46

Black regiments: 1st Kansas Colored Volunteers, 27; 2nd U.S. Colored Artillery (Lt.), 63; 3rd Regiment Louisiana Native Guards, 93–94; 3rd South Carolina Infantry, 30; 3rd U.S. Colored Infantry,

Black regiments *(cont.)*
57; 4th U.S. Colored Infantry, 62; 5th U.S. Colored Cavalry, 134, 156; 6th U.S. Colored Cavalry, 134; 9th Louisiana African Descent, 97, 98, 99; 11th Louisiana Infantry, 98, 99; 22nd U.S. Colored Infantry, 56; 26th U.S. Colored Infantry, 58; 33rd U.S. Colored Infantry, 172; 44th U.S. Colored Infantry, 51, 160; 54th Massachusetts Infantry, 28, 30, 53, 100–102, 105, 106, 114, 116, 154; 55th Massachusetts Infantry, 28, 30, 69, 77, 124–26; 57th U.S. Colored Infantry, 60; 107th U.S. Colored Infantry, 61; 116th U.S. Colored Infantry, 174; 124th U.S. Colored Infantry, 139; black soldiers transferred to from white units, 25n; postwar demobilization of, 49, 157; Wild's African Brigade, 13

Black soldiers: allegedly abuse and pillage after war, 166; combat duty of, 37; continue in army after Civil War, 46; differences among, 36; as difference between victory or defeat for North, 24; background of, 35; bravery of, 94–96, 102, 133, 135–36; want privileges of citizenship, 141, 144–47; condolences to mother of dead soldier, 128–29; deaths of, 126, 128, 156; diet of, 36; want discharge after war, 159–60, 160, 170; endangered after war, 49; enthusiasm of grows with Union's commitment to freedom, 33; should be treated equal with whites in army, 91–92; faithfulness of not repaid with promises made, 174–75; families of suffer, 19, 42, 138–39, 159, 170, 170–71, 175; families of driven away by slaveholders, 137, 138, 160; families of freed by Congress, 21n; want families liberated from slavery, 131–32, 132–33, 140; forgotten after war, viii; guard duty by, 42, 43, 154; hope of from service, 24; hope for equality, 24, 40; illustration of liberating slaves, 76; enjoy feeling of liberators of slaves, 43–44; illustration of marriage of, 78; mistreated by regiment commander, 174; high morbidity of, 34; illustration of mustering out of, 79; mother asks for son's release from army, 136–37; as noncommissioned officers, 36; and black and abolitionist newspapers, 44–45; numbers of compared to states' slave and free black male adult population, 16–17; performed honorably,

114–16; perspective is broadened by military service, 39; philanthropic societies aid, 44; photographs of unidentified soldiers, 69–71; postwar leadership role of, 46; praise of, 86; prejudice against dispelled by bravery of, 133, 135; protect former slaves after war, 46, 158; protest discrimination within army, 26, 34, 35, 45; uncertain whether they will fight effectively, vii, 33, 94, 147; as cause of racial friction in South, 167; refuse lower pay, 29–30; self-esteem of raised by military experience, 38; slaveholders upset with unsettling effects of, 48–49, 164–67; slaveholders condemn after war, 49; and slaves, 44, 48–49; transferred from white to black units, 25n; violence between white civilians and, 49; well armed in South, 165; willingness of to fight, 94; work as laborers, 18, 34, 87, 88, 89, 111–12. *See also* Contrabands; Army, Union

Black women, 43–44. *See also* Families of black soldiers; Rape; Whippings

Border states (Maryland, Delaware, Missouri, and Kentucky): black enlistments weaken slavery in, 1; families of black soldiers remain in slaveholders' custody, 116–17; families of black soldiers in suffer, 42, 137, 138; fertile ground for recruitment of blacks, 15; number of blacks in, 15; number of blacks from in army, 20; slave enlistees receive their freedom, 1

Bounties: black soldiers should have equality of in army, 91–92; larger are promised than given, 152; not paid, 175

Brisbin, James S., 134; letter from, 134–36

Brooks, Colonel, 155

Burbridge, Stephen G., 134

Bureau of Colored Troops, vii, 13

Butler, Benjamin F.: arms free blacks and favors black enlistment, 9; musters in La. Native Guard units, 26–27, 93; accepts black officers, 93; grants asylum to runaway slaves, 3–4; opposes enlistment of runaway slaves, 9

Butts, Major, 112

Cameron, Simon, 85

Camp William Penn, 58

Chaplaincy: commissions issued to blacks for, 121

Childs, Amelia, 173

Childs, Roda Ann: affidavit of, 172–74

Choctaw (gunboat), 98, 99

Citizenship: and discrimination against free blacks in North, 7; emancipation as beginning of responsibility of, 155; gaining rights of as reason for black enlistment, 22; military service of blacks advances claim to, 2; black Tennesseans seek privileges of, 141, 144–47. *See also* Suffrage

Clothing: and discrimination in allotment of for black soldiers, 32, 114

Coburn, Carrie, 108

"A Colored Man," 109–11

Commissioned officers: blacks lobby for, 28; blacks denied opportunity to become, 2, 26, 31–32, 40, 45, 92, 109, 111; blacks not thought qualified to serve as, 27; free blacks lead demand for black commissioned officers, 35, 121; letter from black officers in Louisiana Native Guards, 93–94; black chaplains and surgeons commissioned, 121; and selection of white officers for black regiments, 13; black recruiters commissioned in 1st Kansas Colored Volunteers, 27; blacks serve as in Louisiana Native Guard, 27, 92–93; black officers cashiered out of Louisiana units, 120; reasons why white officers serve in black regiments, 31; War Department opposes black officers, 27–28, 40, 120–21; white officers in Louisiana are slaveholders, 110; white officers of black regiments ridiculed, 134–35

Confederacy: debate in over black military service, 22; number of blacks from in Union army, 20

Confiscation acts, 4, 6, 6n

Congress: backs Butler's policy toward runaway slaves, 4; and conscription, 11; equalizes pay of black and white soldiers, 30, 126; moves slowly toward emancipation, 8; frees families of black soldiers, 21n

Connecticut: Stanton authorizes raising black regiments in, 12

Conscription: abusive, 20; black men in Union states subject to, 19; can buy way out of service, 14; hardship exemptions, 14; in North, 11; opposition to, 14; argument that slaves should be drafted into Confederate army, 103–4

Contrabands: black soldiers guard camps of, 42, 43; definition of, 4; free black men do not want to be considered as, 116; camp near black soldiers for protection, 137; needed as laborers for army, 88; rescued out of slavery by Union laborers, 129–31; U.S. policy toward, 13

Copperheads: definition of, 119; threatened by black soldier, 133

Davis, Jefferson: letter to, 103–4; threatens to treat black POWs as slaves, vii, 105, 118

Delany, Martin R., 12; photograph of, 67

Demobilization: of black regiments after war, 49, 157. *See also* Mustering out

Dennis, Elias S.: letter from, 97–99

Diet: of black soldier, 36. *See also* Food

Diggs, Kitty, 131, 133: letter to, 132–33

Discipline, military: and discrimination against black soldiers, 32

Disease: as cause of death of black soldiers, 126; immunity to, 36

District of Columbia: emancipation in, 5

Douglass, Charles R.: photograph of, 53

Douglass, Lewis H.: photograph of, 52

Downing, George T.: letter to, 91–92

Draft. *See* Conscription

Education: of blacks in army, 2, 40, 154, 161; importance of to blacks, 161; photographs of black soldiers with teachers and school, 64, 65; school established for black children, 162

Eiland, O. G.: letter from, 103–4

Emancipation: abolitionists advocate, 3, 5; as a beginning instead of an end, 154; as an end and a beginning of responsibility of citizenship, 155; black enlistments demanded by white Northerners after, 7; Congress and Lincoln move slowly toward, 8; Congress and Lincoln make it centerpiece of war policy, 10; effected by enlistment of slaves, 18; families of black soldiers are freed, 21n, 131–32; not goal of war, 110, 151; Mississippi recognizes, 167; new Union goal, 88; growing Northern commitment to, 1, 5; North considers gradual and compensated, 5; only way to preserve Union, 3; proclaimed in Florida, Georgia, and South Carolina, 83; should be purpose of war, 5. *See also* Slavery; Slaves

Emancipation Proclamation, 21; black minister's interpretation of, 149; black soldiers grateful for, 141, 144; black enlistments stimulated by, vii, 88; breadth of, 6n;

Emancipation Proclamation (cont.)
illustration of celebration of led by black soldiers, 75; difference between preliminary and final versions, 10; preliminary proclamation, 6; rumor Lincoln will reverse, 106; will help South come back into Union, 151

Enlistment of blacks: citizenship rights as reason for, 22; demanded by white Northerners after emancipation, 7; encourages movement to emancipate slaves in South, 1; enthusiasm grows with commitment to freedom, 33; force used to obtain, 2; freedom as main reason for, 21; growing demand for, 10; by David Hunter without War Department authorization, 83; as lever against slavery and racial discrimination, 8; manpower needs of army provide leverage for, 10; timing of, 32–33; white officers initially oppose, 3. See also Recruitment of blacks

Enrollment Act of March 1863, 14, 19

Equality: espoused by Founding Fathers, viii; hope for, 24, 40; postwar activities of former white abolitionist officers for black equality, 47; should serve in army on basis of, 91–92; War Department cannot guarantee for blacks in military, 30; Northern whites do not contemplate as a result of black enlistment, 25

Equipment, military: and discrimination against black soldiers, 32; black soldiers should have equality of in army, 91–92

Families of black soldiers: abuse of, 117, 118, 156–57, 172, 172–74; affected by military service of, 42; endangered, 49; freed by Congress, 211n; freed from slavery, 131–32; slaveholders drive away, 137, 138, 160; slaveholders punish, 155; stay under custody of slaveholders in border states, 116–17; suffering of, 19, 138–39, 159, 170, 170–71, 175

Fatigue duty: black soldiers work as laborers, 18, 34, 87, 88, 89, 111–12; opposition to assigning black soldiers to do exclusively, 34, 111–13, 113, 126–27

Fisk, Clinton B.: letter to, 161–62, 163

Flags: of 3rd U.S. Colored Infantry, 57; of 22nd U.S. Colored Infantry, 56

Florida: proclamation of emancipation by David Hunter for, 83

Food: diet of black soldiers, 36; short rations for black soldiers, 126, 127–28, 170–71; shortage for families of black soldiers, 160

Forrest, Nathan B., 118, 120

Fort Corcoran, Va., 61

Fort Lincoln, D.C., 62

Fort Pillow, Tenn., 30, 118, 119, 120

Fort Wagner, S.C., 14, 37, 94, 100–102, 106, 115; illustration of assault on, 74; and black prisoners of war, 105

Fortress Monroe, Va., 3

Founding Fathers: espouse equality of man, viii

Frazier, Garrison, 148–53

Free men of color: enlist in Union Army, vii; have different aspirations from slaves, 35; lead demand for black commissioned officers, 35; lead demand for equal pay of black soldiers, 35; in Native Guard units, 3; oppose enlistment in Confederate army, 23; reluctant to enlist, 19; South countenances military service by before North, 23; have tradition of protest in North, 40

Freedmen's Bureau, 47, 161; affidavit to, 172–74; letter to, 167–69

Freedpeople: abused after the war, 158; must be disarmed in South, 167; establish school, 162; forced to work for whites or be charged with vagrancy, 168n; illustration shows welcome of black soldiers in Charleston, 77; learn from free men of color to protest properly, 40–41; importance of marriage to, 154, 155; military victories bring large numbers of under Union protection, 14; photograph of with black soldiers, 65; often take more overt action than free men against army's discriminatory policies, 35–36; poverty of, 10; restrictions put upon in Mississippi, 167; should have all rights of whites, 168; rumor of uprising of against whites, 164–65; black soldiers protect after war, 46, 158, 164–66; terrorized by ex-Confederates, 167–69

Freeman, G. H.: letter from, 128–29

Georgia: blacks in support Union cause, 151; number of blacks from in Union army, 20; proclamation of emancipation by David Hunter for, 83

Gettysburg, battle of, 14

Gibbons, Charles W.: letter from, 93–94

Gillmore, Quincy A.: and Fort Wagner, 100–102; letter to, 158; questions ability of blacks to fight, 100

Gla, Adolph J.: letter from, 93–94

Glasgow, Colonel, 99

Glover, Martha: letter from, 117–18

Glover, Richard: letter to, 117–18

Gooding, James Henry: letter from, 114–16

Gordon, George H., 100

Grant, Ulysses S.: letter to, 89–91; puts black soldiers into battle, 37

Grinnel, Joseph H., 124

Guard duty: by black soldiers, 42, 43, 154

Guerrillas, Confederate, 131n

Haiti, 165

Halleck, Henry W.: letter from, 89–91; letter to, 87–88

Hallowell, Edward N., 102

Hardin, William: letter from, 93–94

Harris, Adam, 140

Harris, Joseph J.: letter from, 140, 142–43

Hawes, James M., 99

Helen, Eli, 162

Higginson, Francis L., 102

Hodgkins, Theodore: letter from, 118–20

Holly, Calvin: letter from, 167–69

Horton, General, 158

Howard, Joseph W.: letter from, 93–94

Hunter, David: letter from, 84–86; supports black enlistment, 8–9, 83; organizes black regiment, 26; proclamation of emancipation by, 80

Impressment: by Union army, 19, 20

Ingram, Joseph, 162

Insurrection: fear of used by ex-Confederates to restrict freedpeople, 167, 169

Irby, Ellis, and Mosley (Miss. legislators): letter to, 164–66

Jackson, Andrew, 93

Jackson, Samuel, 129

James Island, S.C., 72, 101, 102, 115

Johnson, Andrew, 166; letter to, 174–75

Johnson, Hannah: letter from, 106–8

Johnson, Lewis, 160

Johnson, Reverdy: advocates retaliation for Confederate murder of black prisoners of war, 119–20

Jones, John, 12

Justice, military: and discrimination against black soldiers, 32

Kansas: black regiments in, 9, 11

Kelley, J. M.: takes affidavit of widow of black soldier, 156–57

Kentucky: number of blacks from in Union army, 20, 155; recruitment in of blacks for Union army, 134. *See also* Border states

Kirkwood, Samuel J.: letter from, 87–88

Laborers, black: black soldiers work as, 18, 34, 87, 88, 89, 111–12; Union army needs more, 18, 87, 88, 89; Union workers rescue family members out of slavery, 129–31

Land: cheap government land disappearing, 172

Lane, James H.: wants to raise black regiment, 8; favors commissioning black officers, 27

Langston, John Mercer, 12

Lauence, Samuel: letter from, 93–94

Leach, Julius, 156

Leach, Patsey: affidavit of, 156–57

Lee, Andrew, 158

Leib, Herman, 97, 99

Lexington (gunboat), 99

Lincoln, Abraham: election of as president, 151; slowly moves in favor of black enlistment, 11–12; slowly moves toward emancipation, 8; urges slave states in Union to emancipate their slaves, 5–6; letters to, 106–8, 114–16, 136–37; petition to advocating equal pay, 124–25; rumor he will reverse Emancipation Proclamation, 106; urges La. unionists to extend suffrage to black soldiers, 48; threatens retaliation against Confederate prisoners of war, 30, 108, 118, 120; voids David Hunter's emancipation proclamation, 83. *See also* Emancipation Proclamation

Literacy: increases through service in army, 40, 161

Littlefield, Colonel, 102

Louisiana: black regiments in, 9, 11, 26, 37, 59; black recruitment in, 15; areas of exempted from Emancipation Proclamation, 6n, 109; number of blacks from in Union army, 20; black officers in Native Guard units, 27, 28, 92–93; unionists in urged to extend suffrage to black soldiers, 48. *See also* Milliken's Bend, La.; Port Hudson, La.

Lynch, James, 150n, 153

McCullough, Henry E., 99

McMeail, Sergeant: letter from, 174–75

Marriage: black soldier's certificate of, 80; illustration of ceremony, 78; importance of to ex-slaves, 154, 155; order authorizing approved ministers to perform for blacks, 154n

Martin, Sarah, 156

Massachusetts: Stanton authorizes raising black regiments in, 12

Medical care: and discrimination against black soldiers, 32
Miami, 66
Militia Act, 6, 21n, 29, 113
Miller, George, 138
Miller, Joseph, 138–39
Milliken's Bend, La., 14, 37, 94, 97–98
Mississippi: number of blacks from in Union army, 20; recognizes emancipation, 167; restrictions on freedmen in, 167
Mississippi River, 103, 110
Missouri: number of blacks from in Union army, 20. *See also* Border states
Moore, James E.: letter from, 93–94
Moore, William: letter from, 93–94
Morbidity: high rates for black soldiers, 34
Morris Island, S.C., 112, 171
Morton, Oliver P., 121
Mosely, Dr., 166
Mustering out: black soldiers want discharge after war, 159–60, 160, 170; illustration of, 79; mother asks for son's release from army, 136–37

Navy, Union: and bombardment of Fort Wagner, 100–101; gunboats, 98–99; integration of, 25n; number of black men in, vii, 20n; photograph of black sailors on USS *Miami*, 66
New York: convention of black men advocates black enlistment, 12
New York City: draft riots in, 14
Newspapers: of blacks and abolitionists tie black soldiers with larger community, 44–45
Noncommissioned officers: black soldiers as, 36, 41
North: discrimination against blacks in, 7; number of black men in, 15; number of blacks from in Union army, 20; whites in do not contemplate equality of blacks as a result of black enlistment, 25; whites in fight war for Union, not against slavery, 2; whites in skeptical of wisdom of arming blacks, vii; after emancipation whites in demand black enlistments, 7; praise of regiments from, 37

Officers. *See* Commissioned officers; Noncommissioned officers
Ohio: permission not given to raise black regiments, 12

Paige, Nathaniel: testimony of before American Freedmen's Inquiry Commission, 100–102
Parker, Joseph G.: letter from, 93–94
Patriotism: black ministers willing to sacrifice for, 150–51
Pay: free blacks lead demand for equal pay of black soldiers, 35, 114–16, 124–25; lower for black soldiers, 2, 26, 29–30, 34, 40, 45, 113–14, 124–26, 127; black soldiers should have equality of in army, 91–92; Congress equalizes, 30, 126; effects of unequal pay on families of black soldiers, 42
Phelps, John W.: supports black enlistment, 8–9
Plimpton, Major, 102
Port Hudson, La., 14, 37, 59, 65, 94–96; illustration of assault on, 73
Porter, David D., 98
Pratt, Charles R., 25n
Price, Sterling, 105n
Prisoners of war: Jefferson Davis threatens to treat captured black soldiers as slaves, vii, 105, 118; Confederates mistreat blacks, 30–31, 43, 45, 105, 106–8, 115, 118–20, 133–34, 136; Confederates murder, 30; black soldiers should have equal treatment as, 91–92; Lincoln threatens retaliation against Confederate, 30, 108, 115, 118, 120
Pryor, Hubbard: photograph of, 51
Putnam, Colonel, 101, 102

Randall, A. B.: report to adjutant general, 154–55
Rape, 173
Ratliff, Robert W., 134, 135
Rawlins, John A.: letter to, 97–99
Reconstruction, 48
Recruitment of blacks: agents, 12; assure blacks they will be treated fairly in Union military, 26; best way to enlist blacks, 152; centrally coordinated, 13; letter from recruiter, 94–96; opposed by white unionists of South, 15, 18; in Kentucky, 134; equal pay promised, 29; poster for, 54; in South, 20, 152, 152n
Restieaux, E. B. W., 138–39
Rhode Island: Stanton authorizes raising black regiments in, 12
Rice, Corra: letter to, 131–32
Rice, Mary, 133; letter to, 131–32
Rice, Spotswood: letters from, 131–32, 132–33

Robison, E. S.: letter from, 158
Runaway slaves: granted asylum, 3; called "contrabands," 4; enlist in Union army, 8; declared free, 6; used as confiscated property by Union army, 4; illustration of in Union army, 81; used by Union army to construct fortifications, 5; want to enlist, 18. *See also* Contrabands

Saint-Domingue, 165n
Savannah, Ga.: black ministers of meet with Stanton and Sherman, 148–53
Saxton, Rufus: authorized to raise regiments of contrabands, 9
Segregation: black ministers of Savannah support, 150; after Civil War, viii; in Union Army, 2, 25
Seward, William H.: letter to, 121–22
Seymour, Horatio, 12n, 121
Seymour, Truman, 100, 101, 102–3
Sharkey, William L., 166
Shaw, Robert Gould, 101, 102
Shepley, George F.: letter to, 129–31
Sherman, William T.: black opinion of, 153; instructions to, 85; meets with black ministers of Savannah, 148–53; skeptical of black enlistment, 13
Shorter, John F.: petition from, 124–25
Sickles, Daniel E.: letter to, 170–72
Skinner, John, 123–24
Slave enlistments: emancipation accomplished through, 18; South opposes in Confederate army, 23; not welcomed initially, 2; undermine slavery, 18
Slaveholders: criticism of by black civilian, 106, 108; criticism of by black soldier, 132; drive away families of black soldiers, 137, 138, 160; embittered by war, 155; punish families of black soldiers, 155; threatened by black soldier, 133; unionists exempted from Emancipation Proclamation, 6n; upset with unsettling effects of black soldiers, 48–49; want black soldiers removed from the South, 49, 164–67; want to reestablish a new kind of slavery, 169; white officers in Louisiana are, 110
Slavery: criticism of, 108, 144; black soldier vows to free daughters from, 131–32, 132–33; definition of, 149; black soldier wants family liberated from, 140; growing awareness of evils of, 5; indispensable to Southern war effort, 3, 5; must be destroyed, 109–11; blacks petition to abolish in Tennessee, 141, 144–47, 148; prohibited in capital and in territories, 5; slaveholders want to establish new kind of, 169; whites do not fight war to eliminate, 2

Slaves: deference of toward former slaveholders, 48–49; should be drafted into Confederate army, 103–4; value freedom more than preservation of Union, 110–11; black soldiers as liberators of, 43–44, 76, 129–31; protected by black soldiers after war, 46, 158; freed by Second Confiscation Act, 6n; labor of on home front, 3; military laborers rescue, 129–31; moved away from Union troops, 103, 104, 105; perceive black soldiers as liberators, 44; enlistment in Union army justifies use in Confederate army, 104; Union army should get as many as possible from enemy, 90; Union officers send back to masters, 90; women enjoy no liberating experience like black soldiers, 43
Smith, Daniel W., Jr.: letter from, 93–94
Smith, E. Kirby, 105n
Smith, Major, 100, 102
South: was aggressor in war, 151; black veterans are well armed in, 165; black veterans are cause of racial friction in, 167; countenances military service of free blacks before North, 23; described as volcano waiting to erupt, 165; freedpeople must be disarmed in, 167; slaveholders want black soldiers removed from, 49, 164–67; Union party in is destroyed, 90
South Carolina: black regiments in, 9, 11, 26; proclamation of emancipation by David Hunter for, 83. *See also* Fort Wagner, S.C.
Sprague, William, 121
Spridge, Governor. *See* Sprague, William
Stanton, Edwin M., 90; assures blacks they will be treated equally in military, 26; authorizes raising black regiments in North, 12; authorizes raising black regiments in Union-occupied South, 13; authorizes regiments of slaves, 9; aware of advantages of regiments of slaves, 10; letters to, 84–86, 118–20, 159–60; meets with black ministers of Savannah, 148–53; opposes commissioning of black officers, 28
Stearns, George L.: recruits black men in free states, 12
Stephensen, Sergeant, 123
Stevenson, Thomas G., 100, 101

Strong, George C., 100, 101, 102

Strunke, Elias D.: letter from, 94–96

Substitutes in military service, 14, 19, 152

Suffrage: blacks disfranchised at end of 19th century, viii; Lincoln urges La. unionists to extend to black soldiers, 48; Northern free blacks demand, 7; black Tennesseans petition for, 141, 146–47. See also Citizenship

Swails, Stephen A.: commission of blocked by War Department, 28

Sweeny, John: letter from, 161–62, 163

Taylor, Sergeant: letter from, 174–75

Tennessee: black recruitment in, 15; exempted from Emancipation Proclamation, 6n, 144n; number of blacks from in Union army, 20; blacks petition union convention of for citizenship, 141, 144–47. See also Fort Pillow, Tenn.

Terry, Alfred F., 100, 102

Texas: number of blacks from in Union army, 20

Thomas, Lorenzo: bans excessive fatigue duty of black soldiers, 34, 113; letter to, 134–36; report to, 154–55; and slave enlistments, 13

Thomas, Samuel, 167

Thomass, Corporal: letter from, 174–75

Tod, David, 121; asks to raise black regiments in Ohio, 12

Toombs, Robert, 122

Treasury Department, U.S.: and contraband policy, 13

Trotter, James Monroe: photograph of, 68

Turnbuill, Marther H., 140

Turner, Colonel, 100

Ullmann, Daniel: letters to, 94–96, 140, 142–43; and slave enlistments, 13

Vagrancy, 168n

Vicksburg, battle of, 14, 103

Virginia: areas of exempted from Emancipation Proclamation, 6n

Vogdes, Israel, 100

Volunteers, black: bounties to, 19; broadside ballad honoring, 55; numbers of plummet, 11; War Department hopes to fight war with, 11. See also Black soldiers; Enlistment of blacks

Wade, James F., 134, 135, 136

Walker, William: executed for protesting unequal pay, 30

Wall, O. S. B., 12

War Department, U.S.: cannot guarantee equal treatment for blacks in military, 30; hoped to fight war with small army and volunteers, 10; commitment to black enlistment, 11; creates Bureau of Colored Troops, 13; opposes commissioning of black officers, 27–28, 40, 120–21; provides for lower pay for black soldiers, 29

War of 1812: black service in, 93

Welcome, Jane: letter from, 136–37

Whippings: of widow of black soldier, 156–57; of wife of black soldier, 173–74

White, Garland H.: letter from, 121–22

White, William: letter from, 174–75

White officers of black units. See Commissioned officers

White soldiers: ridicule black soldiers and their white officers, 134–35; prejudice of eradicated when black soldiers perform well, 133, 135

Whiteman, Captain, 130

Wickliffe, Charles A., 84, 86

Wild, Edward A., 100; letter from, 129–31; letter to, 112–13; and revenge of slaves against former slaveholders, 43; and slave enlistments, 13

Wild's African Brigade, 13

Wiley, Warren: whips widow of black soldier, 156–57

Wright, Ruphus: letter from, 122–24

Wright, Elisabeth: letter to, 122–24

Young, Mr., 129